THE
POST-NUP
SOLUTION

THE POST-NUP SOLUTION

How to Save a Marriage
in Crisis—or End It Fairly

TOM GARDINER, JD

CHICAGO
REVIEW
PRESS

Published by Chicago Review Press Incorporated
814 North Franklin Street
Chicago, Illinois 60610
ISBN 978-1-61373-750-7

While the author of this text is a lawyer, this book only presents general legal information. The author discusses concepts in the hope that they will expand existing law so that married people can get the full benefit of the post-nup solution. While the author practices in Illinois, Wisconsin, and other states (with court permission), this book is not intended to provide specific legal advice for any state. In fact, the law of Illinois regarding many aspects of family law changed dramatically during the writing and editing of this book. The legal information provided in this book cannot substitute for the advice of a licensed professional in your state. Law varies from place to place and it evolves over time, frequently setting new judicial precedents at both the state and federal level. You are urged to seek your own lawyer, who will advise on appropriate actions for your personal situation.

Library of Congress Cataloging-in-Publication Data
Is available from the Library of Congress.

Cover design: Rebecca Lown
Cover image: Shutterstock/sprinter 81
Interior typesetting: Nord Compo

Printed in the United States of America
5 4 3 2 1

To my wife, Margaret, and my children, Kate and Alex.
Also, to my parents, Lloyd and Dona, who have a few things
to teach people after being married sixty-two years.

Contents

Introduction

Post-nuptial agreements, or post-nups as I'm going to refer to them throughout these pages, can have an enormously positive effect both on marriages and divorces. They can save troubled relationships by facilitating communication and motivating behavioral change; and when the marriages can't be saved they can make divorces less stressful, less costly, and more fair.

Most of you have heard about pre-nups, but a post-nup is probably an unfamiliar concept. Pre-nups are legal documents entered into before the marriage. Typically, they are used by high-net-worth individuals to protect their wealth; an aging, affluent movie star may insist that his younger, poorer wife-to-be sign a pre-nup that limits the settlement she'll receive if the marriage fails. These pre-nups have been subject to a lot of controversy and may be discarded by the courts if they don't meet certain requirements or if someone signed the agreement under duress.

My focus is legal agreements created after the marriage takes place—sometimes five, ten, or more years into the marriage. These post-nups serve both spouses rather than one of them, and they have the benefit of being written after couples are aware of the issues that threaten their marriage. Essentially, they are collaborative agreements about areas of conflict and counterproductive marital behaviors—drinking to excess, infidelity, and more garden-variety transgressions—that lay out plans to help spouses change these behaviors. To provide motivation to change, the post-nup uses negative sanctions—unfavorable adjustments to maintenance, marital property division, and other settlement issues if spouses don't change and a divorce ensues.

Post-nups consist of three sections: the Action Pact, the Custody Pact, and the Property Pact. The Action Pact is all about conduct—the problematic behaviors couples must discuss and one spouse (or both) must change in order to save the marriage. The Custody and Property Pacts are designed to forge agreements on issues such as visitation and division of marital property if the marriage can't be saved.

Post-nups aren't new, but they have not been used very often by couples, in part because of a lack of awareness of what they are and the benefits they provide. They also haven't been used because in the past, marital issues were simpler—as I'll demonstrate throughout the book, the increasing complexity of marriages and divorces makes post-nups far more relevant today than they could have been even ten years ago.

Some courts will be reluctant or constrained by case law or public policy to consider the validity of post-nups. While most states will enforce provisions relating to distribution of assets as long they are fair, some states have hang-ups regarding agreements that mention offending conduct—use of drugs, alcohol, infidelity, and the like; those courts oppose these provisions on the theory that they introduce fault into divorce (most courts do not require a determination of fault as a prerequisite to divorce). Another argument against this concept: courts shouldn't inspect private relations between couples. A third objection: discontinuation of illegal drug usage can't be a consideration in an agreement because citizens have a duty not to engage in crimes.

Let's examine the "fault" objection. I'm not arguing for reintroducing fault into divorce, or suggesting the reintroduction of fault into the courts, or asking the court to peep into the bedroom. Instead, I'm suggesting that the problems that drive couples to divorce can be placed on a written page and that fair agreements between spouses triggered by conduct should be enforced. Spouses give each other ultimatums daily—fix X or we're done.

For instance, a spouse says that if you have another affair/keep drinking/gamble/overcharge our credit card, I will divorce you and see you in court. In a post-nup, the spouse has an agreement with terms for the divorce. Will the judge look at what the parties agreed to when they wanted to save the marriage or ignore that in favor of starting at square one? Will some judges consider accepting conduct triggers (if some case law is against them) when faced with this choice? In states that are hostile to this concept, will legislators think about changing the law to permit such post-nups in the interest of helping marriages survive? In our view, most judges won't want to throw the baby out with the bath water. If the agreement is fair—no matter what the trigger—judges will want to consider the terms of the agreement. Despite our belief, some judges in California have done exactly that: refusing to review the terms of the post-nup because conduct was used as a trigger.

A Pennsylvania court, however, believes that post-nups can reflect reality. In the Laudig case, the stated trigger was the wife's infidelity. As the court stated, "If . . . property rights can be transferred without providing any reason to support the transfer, there should be no reason why a transfer would be invalid if it be conditioned on the occurrence of a specified type of conduct."

Post-nups can work even in states that refuse to consider post-nups that mention conduct. If the state does not want to see conduct in writing, then the parties can simply write the post-nup mentioning conduct that is to be addressed without delineating explicit triggers. In some negative-nup states, parties may agree verbally that if X occurs, they'll divorce and then refer to their fair post-nup agreement that they created when they wanted to save the marriage. Pursuing an even more conservative strategy, couples can simply agree to post-nups that are essentially settlement agreements, to be activated if and when they decide to divorce. Since either party always has the right to file for divorce, the post-nup that excludes conduct achieves the same purpose as one that includes it: to have the spouses agree to reasonable terms for their divorce when they still want to make the marriage work.

Other states may be hung-up on whether the post-nup is prepared in contemplation of divorce or whether they are designed to facilitate a reconciliation. Our post-nups are designed to save marriages. They can be named "reconciliation agreements" in some states and language included specifically to address the concerns voiced in these states.

A growing number of lawyers are recognizing the utility of post-nups in addressing behaviors. For example, a 2015 survey of the American Association of Matrimonial Lawyers revealed that 7 percent of those preparing post-nups addressed infidelity. We think that an increasing number of courts will recognize the value of the post-nups and that the trend will be to enforce these agreements as more are presented to the court. This is an evolving area of law. I am not attempting to create specific post-nups that will work in your state, but only presenting this dynamic concept for you to tailor to your needs and circumstances (i.e., the laws of your particular state). Addressing the laws in each state would make this book a tough slog (you don't want to read about all the variations in the forty-nine states in which you don't live), so as you prepare your post-nup, you should consult a local lawyer.

Still, if you take a historical look at divorces, you find post-nups popping up here and there. Most famously, Donald and Ivana Trump divorced in 1991, but in 1987, ten years after their marriage, they had created a post-nuptial agreement in which Donald would pay Ivana a lump sum of $10 million plus maintenance upon divorce, and in exchange Ivana would agree to refrain from any public discussion of their marriage, Donald, or his business dealings. When Ivana filed for divorce, she asked the court to declare this "publicity" provision unenforceable as a result of "fraud and overreaching." The court, however, upheld this provision.

Now consider another couple (a composite based on a number of couples) and how they used a post-nup. Roger and Margie have been married for twelve years, and after Roger lost his job a few years ago, his occasional drinking spiraled into alcoholism. This has created major problems in their marriage, leading Margie to suggest that they hammer out an agreement—a post-nup—that will deal with these issues. During their discussion about Roger's drinking, Margie proposes a number of options designed to get Roger to stop drinking. Though Roger is resistant at first and in denial about how much of a problem his drinking poses, he eventually agrees to two conditions in the post-nup. First, he must enter weekly counseling with a therapist who is an expert at treating alcoholics. Second, he must join Alcoholics Anonymous and attend meetings regularly. The post-nup creates a series of goals that Roger must meet—staying sober for three months, six months, and a year—and if he meets these goals, Roger and Margie agree to review the post-nup and determine if it makes sense to cut back or stop the private therapy sessions. The post-nup also states that if Roger does start drinking again, he agrees to move out of their residence and into a rehab facility for alcoholics. If he continues drinking after this, a divorce will ensue and, as part of the post-nup agreement, he will not be allowed to see his children without an independent supervisor until he can demonstrate that he has been sober for six months.

Though many post-nups focus on the bad behavior of one spouse, post-nups can include behavioral provisions for both spouses. In this instance, Roger and Margie included a provision in which Margie agrees to be more supportive and less critical of Roger. Roger complained that he drinks in part because Margie frequently makes critical comments to him and others about his inability to keep a job, his weight gain, and other issues. For this reason, the post-nup states that Margie agrees to make a commitment to be more supportive and less critical (in measurable ways), and that if she fails to honor this commitment, she will agree to give Roger a larger percentage of the split of their property if they divorce.*

Though post-nups are more detailed and complex, this brief example provides a bare-bones description of what the process entails. Perhaps just as important as that description, I should provide a bit of background about myself, how I learned about the post-nup, and why I feel so strongly about it.

Contrary to what you might think, I'm not a divorce lawyer. In fact, it's unlikely that a family law practitioner would write this book. Rather, I'm a trial lawyer with a medium-sized Chicago firm. Though I primarily handle business, injury, and municipal cases, some of our lawyers are divorce specialists and, on rare occasion, I'm called in to help. Most of my time over the last twenty-five years of our firm's existence, though, has been spent doing business deals, handling litigation, and forging partnership agreements; I'm outside counsel for 120 businesses.

In the course of working for these companies, I create partner contracts that often go on for forty or more pages, laying out the rules that govern the operation of the business. Clauses address

---

* Some lawyers believe that post-nups involving conduct are far more likely to be enforced if all requirements are mutual.

everything from conflict resolution to steps for dissolution. In many instances, it takes months to hammer out these agreements.

It struck me that from a social point of view, marriage is more important—and arguably more complex—than any business alliance. Yet couples marry with no formal agreement to guide them going forward. Their wedding vows involve informal promises that have no legal weight and are usually not relevant to disagreements that occur later in a marriage. In the past, marriages often had informal but powerful rules—social norms and religious laws created behavioral boundaries that many couples observed. Today, however, these rules have been weakened. Religion has less influence over our lives and we live in a less puritanical culture than in the past—our society is more permissive of all types of behavior. I'm not suggesting this is a bad or a good development, only that it makes a more compelling argument for a formal set of rules to govern the marriage.

For instance, a couple marries and the spouses have two different religions. When they marry, they don't think it's a big deal—they don't plan to have children for a number of years, and when they do, they intend to expose them to both their religions but not force either one on them. When the wife becomes pregnant, however, her parents become insistent that they raise the child in their religion. The wife is inclined to go along with her parents' wishes, but her husband is adamant that they stick to their original plan. This couple could use a post-nup to set the rules about how they raise this child as well as any future children.

Or consider a husband who starts racking up large amounts of debt. His wife didn't realize he was a spendthrift when they married but this behavior has spiraled out of control three years into the marriage. She's tried to talk to him about it, and he promises to stop this behavior—a promise he keeps for a little while and then breaks. If he doesn't stop spending, they will lose their condo and have to declare bankruptcy. He is in denial about this happening and the only way she can shake him out of this denial is via a post-nup: she insists they create a document that states if he cannot curb his spending, they will divorce and he will have to pay her back every penny that he has wasted.

Throughout the book, I'll provide many examples like these, illustrating the different ways post-nups can be used. Some of these examples will be drawn from real couples, some of whom lawyers in my firm have represented and others who have been represented by other lawyers. In all these examples I've changed the names, because post-nups deal with highly personal issues and the bad behavior of one spouse is often the centerpiece of these cases. Other examples are taken from public records—public filings for divorce that describe the post-nups that were integral to settlements regarding property, maintenance, visitation, and other issues. And I've also created examples to illustrate key points about post-nups—examples that reflect emerging issues in marriages and divorces. These hypothetical examples are necessary not only to demonstrate the broad applications of post-nups but because many real post-nups never see the light of day. When post-nups work and save marriages, they never become public the way post-nups that orchestrate divorce settlements do. They may be written on a yellow legal pad by a couple, vetted by a lawyer, and then locked away in a drawer, their mere existence enough to change one spouse's behavior and put the marriage back on solid ground.

No doubt, we're going to see many more examples of post-nups taken out of drawers in the near future, since they have the power to make a generally bad divorce process significantly better. If you have gone through a divorce or know people who have, you are acutely aware of the damage that can be done. Divorces are often highly stressful, expensive, and lengthy. Even worse, if there are kids involved, divorces can be emotionally devastating and end in arrangements that may satisfy one spouse's desire for vengeance but harm the other spouse and the kids.

Part of this book, then, will examine how post-nups can make the divorce process a saner, less emotionally awful experience for both couples and their children.

I should also point out that though post-nups foster collaboration, they are very different from what people refer to as collaborative divorces. This term has received a lot of publicity and the concept is great in theory—it is designed for couples who agree on most issues. A facilitator trained in collaborative divorce helps forge an agreement that the courts can use.

Unfortunately, collaborative divorce happens rarely. In our firm, we have three divorce attorneys who handle many cases annually, and I can count on the fingers of one hand the cases that have been truly collaborative. Too often one spouse decides he's being taken advantage of and tries to "win" more; or what starts out as collaborative degenerates into a battle, because couples divorce for a reason—and the things that destroyed the marriage make it difficult for them to collaborate on anything as significant as a divorce.

If a collaborative couple had a post-nup in place, though, they might either avoid the divorce or at least have clear terms on which they could base a divorce agreement.

Post-nups aren't panaceas. Couples are always going to argue and divorces are always going to happen. Be aware, too, that in some situations, post-nups are not appropriate. First and foremost, when safety is an issue, post-nups may provide a false sense of security. If your spouse is a danger to you or your children, you don't want to depend on a signed piece of paper to protect you. In these cases, use whatever legal means your attorney and the police recommend to protect yourself, from moving out of the residence to obtaining an order of protection to filing criminal charges.

Second, if your spouse is guilty of criminal behavior—tax fraud, for instance—you don't want to put yourself at risk by taking a chance that he'll cease this behavior because of a post-nup.

Third, if you anticipate your spouse's actions will lead the family to financial ruin, don't bet your future on your spouse's promise to stop spending wildly or gambling or doing whatever is draining the family's financial resources.

Fourth, if your spouse agrees to do a post-nup, you hammer out an agreement together, and then she refuses to sign it, view this refusal as a yellow flag. It's possible that while you see the post-nup as a way to save the marriage, your spouse sees it as a delaying tactic—she wants to buy time so she can hide family money in an offshore account or refuses to face facts and admit that her behavior is destroying the relationship. If she postpones signing the post-nup and doesn't suggest new language that she finds acceptable (and that you find acceptable), then she's probably delaying the inevitable.

On the other hand, when couples are having problems but want to save the marriage, they will both be willing to engage in the type of conversations the post-nup catalyzes. It doesn't matter if the problem is serious—drug abuse, marital affairs, drinking, depression—the post-nup provides a forum for couples to air their grievances and reach mutually acceptable agreements about conduct.

This doesn't mean that your spouse will be happy if you angrily shove a post-nup in his face and say, "Sign it!" As I'll discuss, creating a post-nup that works for both of you and presenting it with care are important steps. At the same time, if you follow these steps and your spouse reacts to the post-nup by saying, "Forget it, I want a divorce," then the marriage was doomed and it's better to get out of it sooner rather than later.

So though post-nups aren't one hundred percent effective, they offer a wide range of benefits—benefits that may be directly applicable to your relationship.

The Benefits

How a Simple Legal Document Can
Save a Complex Relationship

W HY DON'T 50 PERCENT of business partnerships dissolve in acrimony and costly legal battles? While professional business relationships are different in many ways from personal ones, they are similar in one key area: clear, mutually agreed upon, formal agreements enhance relationship viability. If people formed companies without a formal, legally binding document, the business divorce rate would far exceed the marital one.

Marriage, like business, is a stressful endeavor. It often begins with great expectations and lofty goals, but over time, tensions mount. Life happens—kids, financial struggles, geographical relocation, jealousy, and so on. Invariably, one or both people in a relationship behave badly, and whether that behavior is justified by the other person's equally bad behavior is irrelevant. We're all human, and we all make mistakes. But these mistakes don't have to doom the marriage.

In a minority of cases, marriages should end. When one of the spouses is an unredeemable jerk, there's not much that can be done.

Sometimes, it turns out that people really are incompatible, and there's no point in prolonging the inevitable.

But many times, good marriages end prematurely. Jack and Jill truly love each other, but Jack had an affair and Jill could not believe his promise that it would never happen again and filed for divorce. Or consider Sue and Sam, childhood sweethearts who married right after they graduated from college and who consider themselves best friends; but after ten years and three children, Sue has had it with Sam's controlling behaviors. Though she tells her friends that Sam will always be her one true love, she is going to divorce him.

A post-nup can save marriages that are fundamentally sound but weakened by bad behaviors. When divorce is inevitable, the post-nup can make the break-up far less emotionally stressful and costly and result in a much fairer settlement.

Let's look more closely at these general benefits so you can understand how a post-nup might apply to your marital situation.

Benefit #1: Sends a Wake-Up Call

People might be in denial about how their behavior is affecting their marriage, and they are shocked when they learn that their spouses have filed for divorce. They rationalize their actions, convincing themselves that their drinking, gambling, inattentiveness, and affairs have less impact on the relationship than they actually do. Men are particularly guilty of being in denial. They tell themselves that their wives will forgive them. They justify their bad behaviors, believing that their spouse "drove" them to do what they did. They may also minimize their neglect or betrayal, certain that an angry spouse will eventually become less angry about something "that really wasn't that big of a deal."

High-net-worth males demonstrate a particular form of obliviousness. Our firm has represented a number of these men, and after they receive the divorce papers, they storm into our offices and fume, saying something along the following lines: "I've given her everything, I've killed myself to provide for my family, she drives a Mercedes, and *she* wants to divorce *me!*"

These individuals need a wake-up call to save their marriages before it's too late, and the post-nup sounds an alarm that's impossible to ignore. Following are some ways it alerts people that their behavior has to change.

• **Cuts through denial with the sharp edge of the law.** Denial is impossible when you tell your spouse that if he doesn't address his "bad" behaviors and discuss them in a legally binding document, then the marriage is over. Whether you present the actual post-nup or introduce the idea of it, both approaches are attention-getting and powerful. Telling your partner that he must consider agreeing in writing to stop using drugs or start looking for a job—and that he faces the potential loss of joint custody* (if the drug usage is to be a basis for challenging whether he should spend unsupervised time with the kids) or some other negative consequence if he fails to adhere to the agreement—will communicate how serious the situation has become. Sometimes, it's useful to present a post-nup as a legal document with your lawyer's name attached, since the official document means that you've gone beyond the talking stage. In other instances, it's better to make the

---

* Many states no longer refer to the primary residential parent as having "custody" of the children, but we use that term because it is most used by laypeople when discussing this issue. We will also use "alimony" for the same reason even though many states use "maintenance," "spousal support," or similar terms.

post-nup a talking point to avoid the anger a legal document can create. You know your spouse, so you should choose the method that is likely to get him to take your concerns seriously without inflaming tempers.

- **Provides therapists with an actionable tool.** Sometimes, therapists are in a good position to send a wake-up call that couples have difficulty hearing on their own. Many people with marriages worth saving see a therapist individually or together. While these therapy sessions may help them vent their emotions and deal with underlying psychological issues, they often fail to save troubled marriages. The problem is that they're all talk and no concrete action. Therapy is designed to provide insight, not a plan with tactics and objectives and accountability. However, combining therapy with a post-nup changes things. A therapist can give patients a tool that helps them take advantage of their insights. In a typical marriage counseling session, a couple may discuss their issues and how what one spouse does bothers the other spouse. With a post-nup, this behavior can be spotlighted in a document and consequences for continuing it can be attached. The discussion in therapy combined with the post-nup action steps can generate the alarm couples need to hear.

As Judy Callans, a Northfield, Illinois, licensed clinical social worker sees it, a post-nup is also therapeutically beneficial because it restores a measure of control to one spouse when the other spouse has been controlling—and destroying—the relationship. "I have a patient who feels victimized by her spouse and weak in the marriage, and the way she responds is by being hostile to her husband. That's not how they restore the relationship. The post-nup can empower her and get them back to a loving relationship. The power in healthy marriages needs to slide back and forth between spouses; one person can't have all the control."

Benefit #2: Catalyzes Difficult but Essential Discussions

Confronting a spouse who is cheating, gambling, drinking, or behaving in other relationship-ruining ways can be hard to do. Sidestepping the problem or talking about it in general terms seems easier in the short run, avoiding emotionally charged conflicts. Unfortunately, these problems usually get worse and eventually end the marriage.

A post-nup, however, is like a fist inside of a velvet glove—it might not seem intimidating outwardly, but it possesses sufficient force to gain everyone's attention. The presentation of a post-nup—with a lawyer or without one—communicates the seriousness of the situation. It focuses the conversation on the specific problem rather than allowing it to spin off on tangential subjects. If you have the document in front of you and read the part of the post-nup that describes the offending behavior and punishment if it's not resolved, you ensure your partner will "get it," that he'll have to face the situation head on.

Some marriages can limp along for years without problematic behaviors being addressed. Consider how a post-nup might engender a discussion about these behaviors. Bill and Rose avoided any mention of his drinking and the problems it caused their marriage. Bill, the child of alcoholics, maintained that unlike his parents, he could control his drinking, in that he never got falling-down drunk and never touched a drop before 6:00 PM. But after that time, he often drank heavily and became belligerent. Some mornings, he couldn't get up in time for work because of bad hangovers, and he lost two jobs because of his tardiness. On a number of social occasions, Bill said things that embarrassed Rose in front of her friends and family. Rose, who was not particularly assertive, had become increasingly unhappy as Bill failed to curb his drinking. Though she "nagged" (Bill's term) him about it, he refused to stop. For a while, Rose told herself that, relatively speaking, things were pretty good—their combined income was decent, Bill was a good father and husband when he wasn't drunk, and he was never physically abusive with her or the children. Bill's drinking went from an irritant to a major issue, but she struggled to do more than merely nag him about it. One day, though, she resolved to present Bill with a post-nup, drawn up by her lawyer a few weeks earlier. At first, he was shocked and angry when Rose gave it to him. Rose's lawyer had instructed her to keep the conversation confined to her requested actions (stopping drinking, attend AA meetings, therapy) and the consequences in the event of a divorce (curtailed visitation, contested joint custody), and she did what he recommended. Suddenly, Bill got it. For the first time in their marriage, he talked to his wife honestly about his drinking and admitted that he didn't know if he could stop. Just talking about it helped Bill be more open about his problem and express his willingness to seek help. Eventually, he was able to cut down on his drinking and then stop entirely.

Benefit #3: Imposes Accountability on Both Spouses

Post-nups contain a "trigger" provision that holds people accountable for their actions in the marriage. This provision states that if you commit act A or fail to do X, a negative divorce settlement result is triggered. If, for instance, your spouse has a drug or alcohol problem and you both agree that he must stop his addictive behavior, violating this provision means he automatically forfeits certain assets that might otherwise be split 50/50.

These provisions put teeth into the promises people make each other about changing their behaviors. Within a marriage, people become accustomed to a lack of accountability. Post-nups change this thinking. When consequences exist for bad behavior or broken promises, spouses think twice about their actions.

In some post-nups, these trigger provisions provide a little wiggle room, recognizing that in some cases, a slap on the wrist can better serve the situation than a more serious consequence. For instance, when the spouse who has been warned about drinking comes home drunk, the post-nup stipulates that he'll receive a lesser penalty for his initial infraction—he has to move out of the house for a month and live with his mother. Then, if he can manage to stay sober, he's allowed to move back home. Escalating penalties can be geared to the number of infractions or the severity of the infraction (one drink versus being falling-down drunk).

Accountability should be a two-way street. For instance, Cyndi creates a post-nup that includes an escalating series of penalties if Frank continues to drink. In their post-nup discussion, Frank says that it would help him a lot if Cyndi was more supportive and acknowledged the stress in his life that causes him to drink. Frank decides he wants to insert language in the post-nup that monitors Cyndi's ability to be supportive versus being a nag, attaching a penalty if she fails to live up to her end of the bargain. Admittedly, quantifying and personalizing terms such as "support" and "nag" can be challenging. Cyndi and Frank did it by listing behaviors for each term: support included behaviors such as expressing empathy when Frank complained about work and not accusing him of being a wimp when he talked about how anxious he was feeling about a health problem; and nagging behaviors revolved around specific, repeated things Cyndi said, such as insisting Frank exercise more when he talked about being stressed out. When both people are held accountable for their actions, the likelihood is that they'll both work to curtail the behaviors that are hurting the relationship.

While a range of behaviors and negative repercussions can be built into a post-nup, a few stipulations can't be included because they will not be permitted by the courts. In some states, the standard percentage of net income paid for child support is 28 percent for two children. Therefore, if Cyndi were to include a provision in the post-nup that dictated Frank would have to pay 90 percent of his income in child support if he started drinking again, the courts would not honor it because of the huge gap between that percentage and what the law dictates. Fairness is important to the courts, and so if a post-nup provision appears to be blatantly unfair, the courts won't enforce it.

For these reasons, it's essential to have a lawyer review the post-nup to determine fairness and compliance with the law of your state of various provisions you agree to. In some states courts, under current law, may be reluctant to enforce post-nups that include conduct clauses. No matter what, the couple will benefit from the accountability that communication regarding expectations imposes on the relationship.

Benefit #4: Decreases Game-Playing

Couples experiencing problems leading up to a divorce often resort to playing games in order to get what they want. These games are destructive to the relationship and turn the divorce process into a nightmare of animosity and costly legal maneuvering. Here's a typical game couples play. Lori and Steve are having trouble getting along and Lori decides to consult a divorce attorney. She tells her lawyer that she can't stand the sight of Steve and needs to get him out of the house. The lawyer explains that Steve has equal rights to the residence and that she can't force him to leave unless he's guilty of "egregious" conduct. A few days later, Lori instigates an argument in which she accuses him of being a failure in his career—Steve was just laid off from a job and he's sensitive about this issue. The argument turns into a shouting match, and Lori provokes Steve to the point that he becomes even angrier and starts insulting her. He threatens to divorce her and hide money so that she won't get any of it in a settlement. He's ranting and raving at top volume, at which point Lori calls the police. When they arrive at the house and ask what happened, Lori says that Steve was "acting crazy" and Steve admits that he was furious and insulting but that "she pushed me past my limit and called you guys to send me a message." Lori hoped that Steve's verbal insults might be sufficient to meet the lawyer's "egregious" trigger for getting him out of the house, but it did nothing more than make a bad situation worse—it made any hope of reconciliation impossible. Steve couldn't get over that his wife called the police on him—neighbors witnessed the police arriving—and his embarrassment and anger resulted in a highly stressful and protracted divorce.

Spouses know each other's pressure points and are often tempted to dig their nails in when the marriage is on shaky ground. When this happens—when they start playing games that inflict pain—the marriage founders. A post-nup provides an alternative for hurtful behaviors. If Lori had known she could create a post-nup, she might have been able to engage Steve in a dialogue about his career problems. She might have felt empowered to insist that he make a good faith effort to get a job, and that if he didn't make that effort, he would have to leave the house for a month. Further, if he failed to take the actions necessary to get back on a career track (and stop moping around and speaking monosyllabically to her and the children), then he would be penalized in the divorce settlement.

There's no guarantee that this post-nup would prevent Lori and Steve from divorcing, but it's likely that it would have provided both of them with a window where they could negotiate and work on finding a solution to their problems rather than enter into a game-playing battle. Hope and reconciliation are possible up to a point in most decent marriages, but once that point is passed and hurtful games start being played, a bad divorce is inevitable.

Benefit #5: Moves couples beyond a moment in time

Marriages falter when couples become obsessed with a particular instance of bad behavior: "You cheated on me with my best friend!" or "You missed our son's baseball game—again!" As understandable as it is to be upset about these misdeeds, couples often lose sight of the larger picture—that an individual and the marriage are more than this single moment in time.

Post-nups allow couples to deepen and broaden the marital discussion beyond this singular moment. During the conversation about the post-nup, both parties have to get past whatever particular offending behavior has endangered the marriage and talk about the larger, long-term issues. The discussion may start with John exploding at his wife, Lois, over some trivial incident; Lois accuses him of being verbally abusive and tells him he was on the verge of being physically abusive. She insists that if they're to stay married, he needs to start anger management therapy and that his agreement to do so be part of the post-nup. He agrees to her requirement but says that she has to spend more time with him and less time watching television when he comes home from work—that he becomes frustrated when she ignores him at night. Consequently, they place a television-watching limit for Lois in the post-nup too. When they talk about the post-nup and how both of their behaviors need to change, they move beyond that one moment in time and discuss the future and the possibility of things becoming better. In this way, the discussion segues from a difficult moment in time to a larger time frame where other situations and options are considered.

Benefit #6: Offers incentives for behavioral change

Marriages often end in divorce because one or both spouses won't change. It's not unusual to talk to people who have been in therapy for twenty or thirty years and hear them say that despite the therapy, they're basically the same person they've always been with the same problems. In marriages, people sometimes make the effort to adjust offending behaviors—they agree to couples therapy, individual counseling, and other approaches—and they may make temporary changes that appease their partners. Sooner or later (and usually sooner), they lapse back into their old patterns and the marriage is destroyed. B. F. Skinner, the famous psychological researcher, conducted a number of experiments that demonstrate how people have great difficulty escaping standard behavioral patterns. Skinner theorized that people change behavior in response to incentives—positive or negative. He called this operant conditioning. The size of the reward or severity of the punishment would depend upon the conduct. To effectuate a small change may require only a small reward or negative sanction. The post-nup is totally consistent with his approach.

I'm not suggesting that post-nups can produce miraculous character transformation, but they do possess the power to alter a particular behavior that is destroying the marriage. They do this in two ways, one negative and one positive. In terms of the former, they create a negative sanction for violating terms of a behavioral agreement—the possibility of seeing kids less or paying more money in a divorce settlement. From a positive standpoint, post-nups force people to confront problems they would prefer to avoid. The guy who is a serial philanderer, for instance, prefers to have a series of affairs rather than talk with his wife about why he continues this destructive behavior. Post-nups create self-awareness and a forum to talk about why he's doing what he's doing. This doesn't mean that he'll change, but it does mean that he's taken the first step to behaving differently. Follow-up therapy and other tools may be required to help him be a faithful spouse, but the post-nup discussion communicates to him that if he wants to save his marriage, this is his best opportunity to do so.

Benefit #7: Sets equitable terms for a settlement if a divorce can't be avoided

When post-nups *don't* save the marriage, they still offer couples the opportunity to negotiate a fair settlement during a time when people are trying to work things out. While one person may be angry with the other during the post-nup-creation period, this anger pales in comparison to the rage that is common during the divorce process. Earlier, couples still possess hope and their goal is to save the marriage—not seek vengeance through the judicial system. They are open to compromise, they are willing to recognize their spouse's good qualities, and they both focus on the best interest of the kids. As a result, the custody, maintenance, visitation, support, and other provisions they include in a post-nup tend to be fair to both adults as well as the kids.

If you believe that this fairness can be maintained during the divorce process, then you probably haven't gone through it (or you're an exception to the rule). People are frequently at their worst during a divorce. I've seen husbands who fight for sole custody even though they don't want it and couldn't handle this responsibility in any case because of the demands of their jobs. I've watched spouses insist on bringing in psychologists who testify that kids bond better with one parent than the other, forcing the spouse to bring in her own psychologist, who makes the opposite recommendation, resulting in a battle that benefits no one, least of all the children. It is impossible to overestimate the amount of rage and recrimination that occurs during a contentious divorce, and so it's far better to settle all the substantive issues before the divorce begins—a post-nup makes this early settlement possible.

Contrary to what you might think, courts do uphold post-nups. Increasingly, they recognize that people often can create agreements about issues such support and property that are fairer than those handed down by a judge who is relatively unfamiliar with a couple and their circumstances. John Winn, an attorney in New York, told me about one of his divorce clients who had a post-nup that was ruled valid by the court. Married for thirteen years with four children, Giovanna Garner and Andrew Garner created a post-nup because of Andrew's drug addiction and an affair he had. The post-nup helped them sustain the marriage for five years, but then Andrew told Giovanna that he had another affair and she filed for divorce because he had violated the terms of the post-nup. Their agreement said that if he violated the terms, he would provide a generous amount of child support and maintenance, give Giovanna the marital home (though Giovanna would be responsible for paying the mortgage), and maintain his life insurance with Giovanna and the kids as beneficiaries. Andrew claimed that the post-nup that he had signed was not enforceable, but the courts upheld it, maintaining that under New York law, a post-nup must "shock the conscience" to be deemed unenforceable.

Some of our proposals in this book would require judges or legislators to expand or change existing laws to enforce the post-nup. To increase the odds that courts will deem your post-nup enforceable, *re-up the post-nup* every few years—re-upping means reviewing the provisions periodically and adjusting them if necessary. Situations change, and the post-nup should reflect these changes. If there is a change in financial circumstances, especially, the post-nup should take this into account, which will increase the odds that the judge will find the agreement fair.

The Advantages in Action

The seven benefits of a post-nup are best appreciated in action. Cognitively, you probably recognize their value as you read, but it's only when you're trying to save your marriage and put a post-nup into practice that these benefits become tangible. That's when the true worth of a post-nup emerges.

To give you a sense of the post-nup's worth in a real-world situation, I'm going to provide a "dramatic" story about how this relatively simple tool might be applied effectively to deal with complex marital problems. I've put dramatic in quotes because marriages frequently unravel with a lot of conflict and emotion, and so I want to portray how the post-nup benefits a couple in the midst of this drama. Bob and Betty were married for ten years, had two kids, and in many respects had an excellent marriage that seemed like it was built to last. Then the marriage hit a major bump in the road, and that bump was big enough to endanger what otherwise was a strong, long-term relationship. One day, while cleaning up their bedroom, Betty discovered receipts for dinner, theater tickets, and a local hotel for a period when Bob was supposedly across the country on a business trip. She confronted Bob, who eventually confessed that he was having an affair with one of her friends. Betty was infuriated and humiliated by Bob's betrayal. She took their children and went to her parents' house across town while she thought about what she should do next.

Over the next several weeks, Bob repeatedly begged her to forgive him and promised he would never again even think about being unfaithful to her. Yet, he resisted her request to go to a marriage counselor because he did not "want to talk about his feelings in front of a total stranger."

Bob wanted forgiveness and to move forward, and while Betty still loved her husband, she was angry and hurt. She began seeing a therapist so that she could think more clearly about what to do next. She wanted to protect herself emotionally and their children financially, but she had no idea how to achieve that goal. While the therapist helped her deal with her anger and guilt (she felt her inattention had contributed to Bob having an affair), Betty remained stuck—she still didn't trust Bob to be faithful and feared the financial difficulties that a divorce would create. Fortunately, Betty's therapist told her about an attorney who did post-nuptial agreements.

They met, and the more Betty learned about a post-nup, the more she was able to see a path forward. She talked with the lawyer about her chief concern—she wanted primary custody of the children and for them to be able to continue living in the home if she were to divorce. The lawyer also said that this provision as well as interim spousal support could be built into a post-nup, but that, in the event of a divorce filing, a judge would determine if the agreement was fair, especially as to the custody arrangements.

Betty had the lawyer draw up the document, and it included a statement in which Bob admitted to the affair and promised to attend couples therapy with Betty for six months and then for additional sessions based on the therapist's recommendation. In exchange, by signing, Betty promised to allow Bob to select the therapist and to not discuss his infidelity outside of their therapy sessions. If Betty brought up Bob's infidelity outside the therapist's office, Bob could skip one therapy session without rescheduling. If Bob missed any sessions without excuse or without rescheduling or was again unfaithful to Betty, Betty would file for divorce. If the filing of divorce was precipitated by additional infidelity or the missing of therapy, or if Bob filed for divorce, the post-nup specified that Betty would receive the house and $2,000 per month for one year as interim alimony or maintenance. The post-nup further specified that, because Bob often worked sixty hours a week, Betty should have primary custody of the children and Bob should have full visitation rights.

Betty took the post-nup to Bob and told him that she wanted him to sign it. At first, Bob was upset and defensive, calling the post-nup "a crazy agreement." But Betty did what the lawyer suggested; she explained that the post-nup was designed to save the marriage, not punish Bob for his past infidelity but motivate him to not make the same mistake twice. "Look," she said, "all you do is say that you love me and that you want to stay together and that you'll never sleep around again, but there are no real consequences if you do. You hurt me, and if our marriage is to work, I need some things from you before I can trust you again. I need to understand why this happened, and I need to see you putting the same effort into our marriage as I do. Unlike you, without these things, I can't move on."

As they discussed the post-nup and Bob thought about what Betty had said, he recognized that the document made sense. While he thought he was capable of being faithful without a Damoclean Sword hanging over his head, he saw why Betty had reason to doubt his promises. He had not realized how serious Betty was about therapy before she brought up the post-nup. He had thought she was demanding therapy as a means to punish him and not because she needed to understand why he cheated. Bob knew a therapist with whom he would feel comfortable discussing his infidelity and marriage. Though Bob at first thought the provisions about the transfer of the house, the spousal support, and the custody of the children were unfair, he realized that from Betty's perspective, they were ultimately irrelevant—he had no intention of allowing his marriage to end in divorce because he cheated on Betty.

Betty had always believed that Bob cared as much about their marriage and children as she did, but the infidelity and Bob's refusal to go to therapy made her question her belief. Now with the post-nup in place, Betty felt more secure that Bob would take his commitment to their marriage and children as seriously as she did. This recognition encouraged her to try to forgive Bob and work things out.

Betty and Bob stayed in their marriage because they loved each other and their family. Together, because they had addressed the real possibility of divorce, Betty and Bob each felt safer to try to work through their differences with more honesty than they had before. If Betty had simply filed for divorce, everything would have been different. A decision would have been made for the future direction of the couple's relationship. Lawyers would be hired to take adversarial positions. Financial information and positions would be exchanged and debated. Custody and visitation would become bargaining chips.

Five years after the post-nup was created, Bob and Betty are still married. Bob has not repeated his infidelity, and he and Betty are much better about communicating their feelings to each other clearly and promptly. They learned in therapy—which lasted almost a year—that they sidestepped conflicts too many times and that these unresolved issues created distance in their relationship. The post-nup opened both their eyes about how openness and honesty would strengthen the relationship, and up to this point, they've taken the lessons learned to heart and their relationship is flourishing.

Assess Your Benefits

Like Betty and Bob, many couples come to a point in their marriage where it's make or break. You may be experiencing this situation now, and if so it's probably because your spouse has done something that has you questioning whether you want to remain married. As difficult as this period is, there's probably still hope, no matter how bad his behavior has been—the marriage can still be saved. At this particular point, it's useful to think about the seven benefits I described and how they apply to your situation. The greater your awareness of the benefit, the more likely you'll be able to take advantage of it.

To that end, I'd like you to think about the following questions related to each benefit and how your answers suggest the value of the post-nup to your marriage:

#1: Sends a wake-up call

- *Are you in denial about your own bad behavior?* Do you rationalize your improper actions? Are you taking actions to undermine your marriage rather than communicate problems with your spouse? On the other hand, are you in denial about how your spouse's behavior is affecting your marriage? Do you tell yourself that his problematic actions or attitude will pass and that he'll change?
- *Do you rationalize your spouse's behavior?* How often do you find yourself justifying what he's doing (e.g., he's under a lot of stress)?
- *How might he react if you presented him with a post-nup?* Would either of you be able to stay in the same state of denial or rationalization about the marriage and its problems?

#2: Catalyzes difficult but essential discussions

- Are there issues in your marriage that you fail to talk about with your partner but wish you felt you could discuss?
- What might your spouse be reticent to discuss that he may be willing to talk about when presented with a post-nup?

#3: Imposes accountability on both spouses

- If your spouse knew he would lose money, custody (under circumstances where the judge believes his behavior might endanger the kids), or something else if he failed to live up to a post-nup's provisions, would he be more likely to do what the marriage needed to survive?
- Would you be willing to make changes in your actions and attitude with similar sanctions and include them in a post-nup in order to help the marriage?

- Would the specific conditions of a post-nup have a positive as well as a negative effect on your spouse? Would he be motivated by your requests to work harder in order to sustain the marriage?

#4: Decreases game playing

- Do you and your spouse know where the other is vulnerable? Do you sometimes take advantage of that vulnerability in order to hurt your spouse (especially after you've been hurt)?
- Do you feel like these painful games are harming the marriage?
- Can you see how a post-nup might serve as an alternative to this game-playing, substituting honest, open discussion for manipulation and combative behaviors?

#5: Moves couples beyond a moment in time

- Is your marriage in trouble because one or both of you are fixated on a single instance of bad behavior? Do all your discussions keep coming back to this behavior?
- Would a post-nup help both of you broaden and deepen your discussion, focusing on the larger issues that are more important to sustaining the marriage?

#6: Offers incentives for behavioral change

- Do you believe that the provisions in a post-nup might help your spouse become more aware of his problematic actions and work harder at changing them?
- Do you believe that the entire post-nup gestalt—the fact that it's a legal document and the discussions that flow from it—can help him focus on what he needs to do to make the marriage work?

#7: Sets equitable terms for a settlement if a divorce can't be avoided

- Do you feel you can make better decisions about custody, finances, and the like when you still have a chance of saving the marriage (versus when you're in the midst of a divorce)?
- Are both of you most likely to consider the interests of your children and the fairness of settlement terms when you're not seeking vengeance or under the tremendous financial and emotional stress of the divorce process?

2

A Flexible Tool

Variations on a Theme

W HAT DOES A POST-NUP LOOK LIKE? In this chapter, I'm going to show you three different post-nups that I've created as samples for our purposes here. One is short, sweet, and written in non-legalese. The second is longer but focuses on a single behavioral issue that threatens the marriage. And the third deals with a big behavioral problem as well as a number of smaller but connected problems.

These three are by no means the only forms post-nups can take. Some people can write their post-nup in the most basic terms possible on the back of a napkin. Others can hire a team of lawyers and produce lengthy legal documents that cover everything from who gets each of the four vacation homes in the event of a divorce to who will pay for the college educations of which children from two previous marriages.

Here, form should follow function. You want to create a post-nup that addresses the particular challenges that you and your spouse face. I've created these three types because they reflect three very different types of relationships—they should help you see the different ways you can structure these agreements. Just as important, they'll help you visualize what a post-nup looks like. In later chapters, I'll focus on specific sections of these agreements. Here, though, is a more general overview of what's involved. Following each one, I'll note what's distinctive about each.

These examples are all informal. The post-nups that we propose are breaking new ground. No doubt, they'll evolve over time and usage. Given that we're in the early stages of post-nups and aren't sure what forms will work best in the future, consult a lawyer if you want to increase the chances of a court ultimately enforcing these agreements.

The first one is short and sweet and thus presented in its entirety.

The Rosenthals' Post-Nup

Post-Nup

This postnuptial agreement is made in New York, New York, this _____ of December, 2016, between MINDY ROSENTHAL and BERTRAM ROSENTHAL.

Recitals

A. We were married on June 15, 2012, in Hudson, New York, where the marriage was registered. It was a wonderful event.

B. We had two children together: Milton Rosenthal, born December 7, 2013, and Stephanie Rosenthal, born July 4, 2015. We haven't adopted anyone. Mindy is not currently pregnant; and we do not anticipate having or adopting any other children, but stranger things have happened.

C. We were both previously married. Bertram has three children by his previous marriage and Mindy has four children by her previous marriage.

D. We want New York law to apply to this agreement.

E. We are making these promises to each other because our marriage needs hope.

Why This Agreement

We love each other but have experienced great difficulties in our marriage. We desire to address those difficulties in this agreement and preserve our marriage. We feel that prior agreements between us have failed because there were no consequences if the promises were not kept. As a result, we agree that the failure to keep certain promises in this agreement will result in a divorce. Furthermore, we realize that we both will be disappointed and may become angry at each other if a divorce is filed. We both realize that we should set out the terms of a possible divorce now when we want to save the marriage rather than during a divorce when we may be looking to hurt or take advantage of each other. Our past divorces were so bitter that the *War of the Roses* movie could have borrowed from them.

Problems Leading Up to This Agreement

There have been lots of problems leading up to this agreement. We have tried our best to address them but we haven't found final solutions.

The problems:

1. Mindy thinks that Bertram's kids hate her. Mindy is not that keen on Bertram's kids, either. Bertram asks Mindy to arrange visitation with his kids through his ex. Mindy thinks that Bertram's

ex is a vindictive, evil person who views Mindy as the house
wrecker who stole her husband.

2. When Mindy's kids are around, Bertram doesn't give them the
time of day. Instead, he plays with his cell phone and watches
the Yankees or Knicks on his iPad.

3. Mindy used to be Bertram's secretary, but she had to quit because
of Bertram's business's antinepotism rule. Now she's stuck at
home with their two kids waiting for him to come home.

4. Bertram's new secretary goes on business trips with him just like
Mindy used to. Mindy is concerned that Bertram might cheat
on her with his secretary. Mindy has gained a few pounds since
having the recent kids. She calls Bertram's new secretary "the
stick" because there is not an ounce of fat on her shapely figure.

5. Bertram works 60 hours a week. He has always done this, but
he promised Mindy that he would cut back once they were
married.

6. Mindy got bored at home. She had an affair with Jack McKiver
when McKiver lost his job. McKiver lives on the same block.
Bertram was irate about this and hasn't trusted Mindy since.

7. Mindy's kids are in college or heading to college. Mindy has
told them that they can go to any college that they want. One
child is a sophomore at Brandeis; another at University of Chicago; and a third has been accepted at Barnard. Since Mindy's ex
doesn't have much money, Bertram is paying over $110,000.00
per year in tuition for Mindy's kids. He thought that would be
okay when it started, but Bertram's stock trading business has
had a tough two years.

8. Bertram likes to use cocaine. Mindy hates all drugs and really
hates Bertram when he uses cocaine. She also hates it when Bertram says that all of the successful traders "do cocaine." Mindy
believes that Bertram is addicted. Bertram claims that he could
stop on a dime—if he wanted to.

9. Most times when the couple schedules counseling, Bertram cancels at the last minute. When Bertram attends counseling, Bertram agrees to every suggestion made by the counselor and then never does any of them.

10. They seem to have no fun together anymore. Bertram works all the time and Mindy takes care of or entertains nine kids sometimes, including trying to meld the family while Bertram seems indifferent.

11. Religion is important to Mindy, but not to Bertram. Mindy feels weird going to temple alone.

12. Mindy thinks that they rarely have enjoyable sex or physical time together. Bertram falls asleep as soon as he gets into bed and awakes and heads to work as if a fire alarm has sounded.

13. Some of Mindy's kids are having real problems with the divorce of their parents.

The Solution, We Hope

We want to reconcile. We are going to honestly address each problem and try to fix them. We are going to hire professionals to help us. We are going to either reach a solution or go our separate ways.

Action

1. Bertram's Ex: Bertram is going to have counseling with his kids. Bertram is going to take his kids and Mindy to a recreational event each quarter to attempt to "break the ice." Bertram is going to make all arrangements with his ex for visitation. Bertram is going to speak highly of Mindy to his kids.

2. Bertram and Mindy will have marital counseling. Bertram will attend all sessions and will engage in the sessions. If Bertram's schedule prevents his attendance at a session, we will reschedule

it in the next ten days. If Bertram misses three sessions in one year, Mindy plans to file for divorce.

3. Mindy will get counseling with her children as soon as possible. Because two are in college, some counseling may be done on Skype. To the extent that Bertram can be part of the counseling, he must attend and the same rules as for marital counseling will apply. Bertram will give Mindy's kids attention when they visit.

4. Bertram will no longer encourage his new secretary to attend business trips. If she has to attend, he will show Mindy receipts to prove that they had separate rooms and will show her both of their expense reports to prove that they did not share private meals together.

5. Bertram says that he can't stop working 60 hours per week and still pay all of his obligations. He will reduce his time at the office to 50 hours per week, but Mindy will accept that he has to work from home for the balance of the time.

6. Mindy has promised that her affair with Jack McKiver is over. Mindy will show Bertram her cell phone every week so that he can review calls and texts. She will also provide Bertram with all pass codes to her e-mail and social media accounts. The marital counseling will address the trust issue. Both of us will agree to participate in assigned exercises diligently and faithfully.

7. Bertram shouldn't be responsible for all of the tuition for Mindy's children. Mindy will tell her children that this is no longer financially possible and that it is not Bertram's fault. Mindy and her children will consider her children taking loans for which they are responsible. As for the child considering attending Barnard College, that child should also apply to state schools. All of Mindy's children will be expected to work during college. Bertram's contribution to the education of Mindy's children will be capped at $40,000.00 per year.

8. Bertram will stop using cocaine. Bertram will stop referring favorably to persons who use cocaine. If he uses cocaine one time after signing this agreement, he must complete an evaluation and rehab program at a Hazelden affiliate. If he does not go for rehab, Mindy will file for divorce. Mindy recognizes that kicking the cocaine habit can be difficult; she understands that rehab may not be totally successful the first time. If Bertram attends rehab, and he uses cocaine thereafter he will go back to rehab for further treatment on one additional occasion. If he uses cocaine after the second rehab, Mindy will file for divorce.

9. Bertram will engage himself in all events seeking to meld the two families. He will make a real effort and will attend and encourage counseling, if unwanted.

10. We will spend physical time together as our mutual trust improves.

11. Bertram is not a religious person. He will attend the High Holidays with Mindy and will attend any temple events involving his children (musicals, plays, and sports).

IF WE DIVORCE

If we divorce:

1. We each have premarital assets that we keep separately.

2. We each continue to have separate bank accounts and credit cards. We will keep these separately.

3. In the event of death, we still want to provide for the children from our first marriages, so we will distribute our assets to reflect this desire, but we will also recognize that the distribution should change over time if we achieve our goal with this agreement and sustain our marriage:

  A. If the marriage lasts less than five years: the dead person's estate pays 15 percent of assets to the survivor.

    B. Marriage lasts five to ten years: 33 percent.

    C. Marriage lasts more than 10 years: 75 percent.

4. Mindy gets 15 percent of Bertram's net salary for three years and nothing thereafter.

5. Our retirement benefits accumulated during the cause of the marriage shall be divided 60 percent to Mindy and 40 percent to Bertram.

6. Child support and where our kids will live: child support shall be provided based upon statutory guidelines. We are both good parents to our children. Mindy will have custody, but Bertram will have visitation during every other weekend and two weekday evenings. Bertram agrees that, if he is still using cocaine, he will only have weekday visitation and it will be in the presence of someone Mindy trusts or will otherwise be supervised. Bertram agrees that he can be tested for cocaine every month upon Mindy's request, but if he is found to be clean, Mindy pays for the test.

7. We will sell our home and split the proceeds equally.

8. Debt: Mindy is responsible for 60 percent of our joint debts and Bertram is responsible for 40 percent.

9. Expenditures on cocaine after this agreement or on affairs will be deducted from that person's share of distributions.

10. Day care: Bertram will pay 75 percent and Mindy 25 percent for the first through third years; 50-50 thereafter.

11. Attorney fees: Each of us will pay for our own attorney's fees.

Bertram Mindy

The Rosenthals' Post-Nup Explained

As you can see, this post-nup covers a lot of ground, but it does so simply and clearly. While our fictional Bertram and Mindy created this document on their own, they would have needed an attorney's advice to make sure that they didn't neglect key points or fashion an agreement that was unfair in any way—problems that could lead a judge to dismiss it. The first half of the document addresses the problems the couple has been having—Bertram's cocaine use, Mindy's affair, etc.—as well as what they hope the agreement will accomplish. The second half states the proposed solution—specific actions that they both agree to take. Some of these actions are accompanied by negative consequences—consequences that are triggered by failure to complete the actions in the manner specified. Finally, the document ends with a further discussion of the consequences if a divorce should take place.

I have not included a penalty provision in this agreement to cover violations of the post-nup. For instance, we could have included that Bertram and Mindy would have to pay a penalty if they failed to live up to the agreement. If Bertram failed to attend counseling sessions three times in a year, Mindy would file for divorce. If Mindy has another affair, her alimony payment is reduced by 5 percent. We did not include these provisions, though, because as of this writing, not every state will respond positively to penalties. We have read cases in New York and Pennsylvania that would suggest that they those courts may have no problem with penalties. Nor would Hawaii based upon a case decided there. A Hawaii court has upheld a post-nup entered into by the spouses in which the trigger to entering the agreement was the wife suspected that her husband was having an affair. More specifically, the wife stated that she suspected an affair because husband had lost weight, was working out, was well tanned, and was giving other women "lecherous looks." The agreement did not specify the trigger, but stated that, if the parties were to separate from each other, certain assets would be disproportionately distributed to the wife.

Even in states that are not receptive to behavioral conduct triggers, there may be ways to use post-nups effectively without them. For example, California courts do not favor conduct-based provisions or penalties based upon conduct, but they do enforce post-nups that contain provisions giving a disproportionate share of the assets to one spouse.

You don't have to follow this form if you decide to create your own post-nup, but you do have to make sure you articulate the problems, the solutions, and the consequences for failing to adhere to the proposed solution.

The Smiths' Post-Nup

Note: This detailed post-nup has been edited in part to focus on the most salient points.

POST-NUP

This postnuptial agreement (hereinafter "the post-nup") is made in Chicago, Illinois, this _____ of December, 2014, between PAMELA SMITH (hereinafter "Wife") and KEITH SMITH (hereinafter "Husband").

RECITALS

A. Three children were born to the parties during the course of their marriage, namely Wilbur Smith, born January 1, 2010; Orville Smith, born March 10, 2012; and Katherine Smith, born July 25, 2013.

B. The parties are making this post-nup because they have experienced martial difficulties and wish to reach certain agreements to eliminate sources of conflict between the parties and promote harmony in the marriage. The parties further recognize that, in the event that harmony cannot be maintained, they are better able to reach reasonable agreements now than when either or both parties has determined that the bonds of matrimony must be dissolved.

ARTICLE I
THE ACTION PACT

1.1 The parties have agreed to the following:

A. Husband has a serious problem with dependency on alcohol. While this has been true throughout the marriage, Husband's problem has gotten worse and he now drinks excessively and frequently passes out in the presence of our minor children. When he is drinking, Husband is noncommunicative with the entire family. Husband agrees that his excessive drinking is harming the marriage and preventing him from acting as a good father. Husband also agrees that he should not be with the children when he is drinking. Husband admits that he has passed out from alcohol when parenting the children.

1.2 Wife and Husband agree that Husband will join Alcoholics Anonymous by _____ and will attend meetings on the following basis: _____

_____

_____

Husband has agreed to complete the 12 Step process by_____, 20____.

Husband agrees to check himself into the Huntington-Ware Treatment Facility for a two-week period beginning Sept. 14.

Husband agrees that he will not drink alcohol nor will he be in the presence of his children were he to drink alcohol.

ARTICLE II
IF WE DIVORCE

In the event of such filing, the remaining terms of this shall bind the parties and shall serve as the agreed terms to be presented to the judge presiding over such proceeding. It is the intent of the parties that such terms be included in the judgment. It is further agreed by the parties that the terms for custody and visitation are agreed to be in the best interests of the children.

ARTICLE III
MAINTENANCE/SPOUSAL SUPPORT UPON DISSOLUTION OF MARRIAGE

3.1 Husband shall pay Wife maintenance in the amount of $_____ per month for a period of two (2) years. Upon the termination of a two-year period, Wife shall be barred from any and all right she has in maintenance and support from Husband, and shall not be able to return to Court requesting the same.

3.2 Husband is currently employed as a managing director for Parker Brothers, as a Monopoly Salesman. Husband has disclosed his current salary to wife. Husband acknowledges that his property and his employment income are sufficient and adequate to support himself. Therefore, he does not require and hereby forever waives any maintenance, formerly known as alimony, or support from wife. Husband agrees that in the event that the parties divorce and any litigation is pending between the parties in any proceeding now or in the future, Husband shall not request any Court to grant him maintenance or spousal support from Wife, temporary, permanent, or otherwise, and he will waive and release all rights and claims to maintenance and support against Wife, including temporary and final attorneys' fees, expert fees, and costs.

3.3 Wife is currently employed part time working 20 hours per week at Walgreens. Wife has disclosed her current salary to Husband.

ARTICLE IV
PROPERTY RIGHTS UPON DISSOLUTION OF MARRIAGE

4.1 If a judgment of dissolution of marriage, divorce, or judgment in any other action between the parties is entered in a proceeding between the parties, upon entry of any such judgment:

A. Division of Property: All property set forth in Exhibit A and property acquired after the execution of this Agreement shall be divided in such manner that Wife shall receive sixty (60%) percent of the net value thereof ("net value" being defined as the then fair market value of such property less the amount of any liabilities associated therewith and any costs of sale) and Husband shall receive forty (40%) of the net value.

ARTICLE V
RETIREMENT BENEFITS

In the event of divorce or the death of either party, the parties hereby agree to the following of any and all right, title, and interest in Husband's qualified retirement plan, 401(k) plan, or employer contribution savings plan, IRAs, pensions, or annuities, accrued during the marriage: fifty-five (55%) percent to Wife and forty-five (45%) percent to Husband. The parties shall cooperate in executing the necessary documentation to effect such a division, including a QDRO letter of direction, or other required document.

Article VI
Custody and Visitation

6.1 The parties agree that, if Husband can discontinue his alcohol intake, they both are fit and proper persons to have the care, custody, control, and education of the minor children. The parties agree that, if Husband does not discontinue his alcohol intake, that it is in the children's best interest that custody be awarded to the Wife.

6.2 The parties agree that, in the event that Husband does not discontinue his alcohol intake, the minor children should have supervised visitation for the Husband because of Husband's alcohol problem.

Article VII
Medical and Life Insurance, Day Care, and Extracurricular Costs

7.4 The parties shall equally split (50/50) all of the costs associated with a child's schooling (i.e., registration, book fees, uniforms, etc.) as well as all costs associated with extracurricular activities. The parties will consult with one another when making decisions regarding a child's extracurricular activities, and neither party shall enroll a child in an activity that costs over $100 without notice and the consent of the other parent. Neither party shall unreasonably withhold consent for a child to be involved in said activity.

The Smiths' Post-Nup Explained

Unlike the previous Rosenthals' post-nup, this one revolves around a single issue: Keith Smith's drinking problem. The Rosenthals both had counterproductive behaviors that the post-nup addressed; here, the document's triggering behavior is Keith's drinking. As the Action Pact section of the post-nup points out, if Keith doesn't attend his AA meetings or continues to drink, Pamela will institute divorce proceedings, he will lose custody, and his visitation will only take place under supervision. These are powerful incentives for Keith to work hard and save the marriage. Perhaps more important, the post-nup spells out both the old behaviors that Keith must stop and the new behaviors he must adopt. This specificity within a legal document is highly motivational. From a practical standpoint, it makes what it will take to save the marriage crystal clear. From a purely psychological standpoint, it demonstrates Keith's and Pamela's commitment to try to make the marriage work.

Clearly, this post-nup is more formally legalistic than the previous one. This is appropriate, in that Keith needs a wake-up call, and a legal document that outlines the situation in detail and the consequences if he continues his harmful behavior will get his attention. Though not all the details of the post-nup are displayed here—the full post-nup would include everything from who will pay for the children's college education to maintenance to conflict resolution procedures—this sample selection hammers home the reality of life after divorce. The seriousness of the situation, too, mandates pre-divorce agreement on all the key issues. More so than the Rosenthals, the Smiths are likely to get divorced sooner rather than later. Keith's drinking is destroying the relationship. Pamela also knows that if the post-nup can't save the marriage, she can use it to secure agreement on everything from custody to visitation to maintenance now, so the divorce will be far less combative, stressful, and costly.

The Jacksons' Post-Nup

Note: This detailed post-nup has been edited in part to focus on the most salient points.

POST-NUP

This postnuptial agreement (hereinafter "the post-nup") is made in Chicago, Illinois, this _____ of December, 2014, between D'LILA JACKSON (hereinafter "Wife") and STEPHAN "SJ10" JACKSON (hereinafter "Husband").

RECITALS

A. D'Lila and Stephan were lawfully married on February 14, 2014, in Versailles, France, where the marriage was registered. Husband is a rap singer and celebrity who is frequently in the public eye. D'Lila is a philanthropist who has a particular interest in children's causes.

B. One child was born to the parties during the course of their marriage, namely N'Tasha Jackson, born January 1, 2015.

C. No other children were born to or adopted by the parties: D'Lila is not currently pregnant; and the parties do not anticipate having or adopting any other children.

D. The parties are making this post-nup because they have experienced martial difficulties and wish to reach certain agreements to eliminate sources of conflict between the parties and promote harmony in the marriage. They are entering this post-nup seeking to continue their marriage and in full expectation that each party will meet the expectations set forth in this post-nup. In the event that such expectations are not met, the parties request that the court enforce the terms of this post-nup because the parties have entered the post-nup with equal bargaining abilities and with full knowledge of behaviors that must be changed for the marriage to continue.

ARTICLE I
THE ACTION PACT

1.1 The parties have acknowledged certain issues that need resolution if the marriage is to continue. The parties have agreed to the following:

A. Husband attended Ripon College and received a degree therefrom. He also studied at the Sorbonne in Paris. His education was financed through loans and credit cards such that he now owes $159,312.00 on student loans and credit card debt.

B. Wife has saved money prior to the marriage and does not favor debt. She has used her premarital funds to reduce Husband's loans to the current level.

C. Husband also has incurred credit card debt totaling $65,700. Husband also owes $120,000 on a car loan for his Bentley and $980,000.00 on his penthouse unit on Park Avenue, New York. Wife has no credit card or other debt.

D. The debt incurred by Husband has caused difficulty in the marriage. Husband has incurred this debt prior to the marriage and after. He has not consulted with Wife before incurring new debt. Furthermore, Husband lied about his debt prior to the marriage. Only when Husband started receiving collection notices and calls at the marital home did Wife learn of some of Husband's debt.

E. Husband has said that the debt should not concern Wife. Husband now admits that the debt is affecting the marriage and that he has disclosed all of his current debts. Husband acknowledges that his debt has high interest rates and that the level of debt makes obtaining new loans at market rates impossible. Husband also acknowledges that he is inclined to "buy now and pay later" and is a compulsive buyer of real estate and personal luxury items. He further acknowledges that, because of the high interest rates that he pays on his debt, he could never catch up and pay off the current loans.

F. Husband further acknowledges that, because his biggest hit has been "Responsibility with a Capital R!" he cannot file for bankruptcy without hurting his reputation among his fans.

G. Wife is agreeable to giving Husband a "clean slate" to see if it will preserve the marriage. As such the parties have agreed to the following:

1. Wife will use her premarital funds to pay off all of Husband's loans, totaling $1,325,012.00.
2. Husband will incur no further debt during the course of the marriage. Husband will be given one joint credit card with Wife, with a limit of $2,000.00 to cover emergency situations when he is on the road. Husband will have no accounts in his own name.
3. The bank account for Responsibility! Rap!, Inc. and any of Husband's other interests, shall now be in Wife's name alone.

4. Title to the Park Avenue penthouse will be transferred to joint tenancy with Husband and Wife. Wife shall have the right to rent the Park Avenue penthouse.

5. The Bentley will be titled in Wife's name. Wife has the ability to sell the Bentley, but must replace it with a vehicle worth at least $40,000.00.

6. Husband will sign a Will and Estate Plan in which all of his worldly possessions, including royalties to his songs, whether now in existence or created in the future, should be transferred to Wife.

7. Wife must approve all purchases of jewelry sought by husband.

ARTICLE II

We believe that giving our marriage a new start will save it. If it doesn't, we have agreed on a fair way to end our marriage within the post-nup. Either of us is free to proceed with a divorce at any time for any reason. Our Action Pact doesn't have to be met before one of us files for divorce. If one of us doesn't satisfy one of the Action Pact items, that doesn't mean that the other spouse will file for a divorce, either.

ARTICLE III
MAINTENANCE/ SPOUSAL SUPPORT UPON DISSOLUTION OF MARRIAGE

3.1 Maintenance from Husband to Wife is reserved for a period of two (2) years. Upon the termination of the two-year period, Wife shall be barred from any and all right she has in maintenance and support from Husband, and shall not be able to return to Court requesting the same.

3.2 Husband is currently employed as a musician for Responsibility! Rap!, Inc. Husband has disclosed his current salary to wife.

Husband acknowledges that his property and his employment income are sufficient and adequate to provide for and to enable him to provide for his support and maintenance. Therefore, he does not require and hereby forever waives any maintenance, formerly known as alimony, or support from wife. Husband agrees that in the event that the parties divorce and any litigation is pending between the parties in any proceeding now or in the future, Husband shall not request any Court to grant him maintenance or spousal support from Wife, temporary, permanent, or otherwise, and he will waive and release all rights and claims to maintenance and support against Wife, including temporary and final attorneys' fees, expert fees, and costs.

ARTICLE IV
PUBLICITY

4.1 Without obtaining the Husband's written consent in advance, the Wife shall not directly or indirectly publish, or cause to be published, any diary, memoir, letter, story, photograph, interview, article, essay, account, or description or depiction of any kind whatsoever, whether fictionalized or not, concerning her marriage to Husband or any other aspect of Husband's personal, business, or financial affairs, or assist or provide information to others in connection with the publication or dissemination of any such material or excepts thereof. Any violation of the terms of this paragraph shall constitute a material breach of this agreement. In the event such breach occurs, the Husband's royalty obligations pursuant to paragraph _____ to make payments or provisions to or for the benefit of Wife shall thereupon terminate. In such event, Wife will sign an assignment of all her royalty interests to Husband. In addition, in the event of any such breach, Wife hereby consents to the granting of a temporary or permanent injunction against her (or against any agent acting in her behalf) by any court of competent jurisdiction prohibiting her (or her agent) from violating the terms of this paragraph.

ARTICLE V
AFTER BORN CHILDREN

5.1 The parties married later in life. Husband is now 45 and Wife is 38.

5.2 Husband has preserved his sperm and Wife has harvested and preserved her eggs.

5.3 In the event of divorce, Wife may still desire to use Husband's sperm to fertilize her egg and produce a child or children.

5.4 In the event that a child is born from Husband's sperm after the date of divorce, Husband shall have no financial obligations and shall have no parental rights with respect to such child or children.

The Jacksons' Post-Nup Explained

Like the Smiths' post-nup, this one is written in a more formal, legalistic style. Unlike the Smiths, though, the Jacksons have complex money and privacy issues. A significant part of the post-nup is devoted to Stephan's considerable debt, incurred both before the marriage and after. He has a problem with money—he spends it faster than he earns it, even though he makes a mid-six figure income. If he wants to remain married to D'Lila, he has to change his spending habits and give D'Lila greater control over and transparency about his finances.

At the same time, this post-nup is a two-way deal. As a rapper who stresses responsibility, Stephan is anxious about D'Lila going public with his money problems. Therefore, as part of the post-nup, a section (Article IV) addresses the issue of "publicity" and prohibits D'Lila from disclosing Stephan's personal, business, or financial situations upon penalty of forfeiting significant financial support in the event of a divorce. This clause provides further incentive for Stephan to stick to his part of the deal, since it suggests that D'Lila has threatened to disclose Stephan's spending habits during arguments.

This particular post-nup also illustrates that a variety of issues unique to a couple can be included in this document. For instance, the "After Born Children" section notes that as an older couple, Stephan has preserved his sperm and D'Lila has harvested and preserved her eggs. If they divorce, this clause grants permission to D'Lila to use the sperm to get pregnant. But it also states that Stephan will not be responsible financially for a child born to D'Lila using his sperm after a divorce.

The Devil Is in the Details

As you read the second and third post-nups, you may have wondered if it was necessary to include all the clauses and sub-clauses. Why not just do the first, simple post-nup or an even simpler version? You can! I'm not suggesting that one type is better than the other. It all depends on your particular concerns and circumstances.

As a general rule of thumb, if you and your spouse are in basic agreement about the issues and they're relatively cut-and-dried, a simple post-nup may suffice. Similarly, if you believe your spouse will be much more amenable to a simple post-nup than a longer, more detailed one, then opt for the short and sweet approach. I've found that some people can't stand wading through long contracts of any type—it's easier for them if they're presented with the shortest possible legal document, written in everyday language.

In some instances, however, you need a longer, more detailed document. Sometimes the issues—especially the financial issues—are complex. Sometimes the enforceability of the document is a concern—you're worried that a judge may be reluctant to sign off on the agreements you and your spouse have made regarding maintenance, property division, visitation, and so on. In these cases, the more detail, the better. In the simple post-nup, you probably noticed that the Action Pact was relatively brief. In the other two post-nups, the actions required by or both spouses are much more detailed. This detail is designed to anticipate what might happen if X takes place. For instance, if your alcoholic husband falls off the wagon and goes on a violent drunken binge, you file for divorce; if he merely misses one AA meeting, then he receives a warning—two warnings and you file for divorce. These "what if" clauses in the post-nups we've featured address uncovered medical costs, retirement benefits, representation on advice of counsel, unborn children, and many other issues.

If judges believe that a post-nup includes all the key points relevant to a given issue, they are much more likely to approve of the post-nup. The detail tells the judges that an issue has been thoroughly analyzed and all contingencies have been covered. As a result, they feel that both spouses understand and have thought through the implications of what they're agreeing to. Post-nups involving conduct are still a new concept for many judges and are not yet accepted by many states. Even shorter post-nups should be reviewed by a lawyer, whose advice can make a real difference in making the post-nup palatable to a judge.

Be aware that the more detailed a post-nup is, the greater potential for argument and negotiation. Think about the post-nups that you just read. They covered a lot of ground in depth—who can disclose what and when about the marriage, who gets the Bentley and the penthouse, how retirement benefits will be divided. Each particular subject raised, though, is a subject that is brought up for debate. If you and your spouse are of one mind on these issues, great. But if you suspect that your spouse will fight you tooth and nail if you try to include certain clauses in the post-nup, you may want to think about how important they are to address now. It may be that it's not worth raising the subject of your spouse's occasional losses in his weekly poker game, as irritating as the loss of money is, if it's not a pivotal issue in your marriage.

Other Variables That Affect Post-Nup Type

Don't look at any of the three post-nups featured in this chapter and say, "This one would be perfect for our marriage." You may find one that seems well-suited to your circumstances, but you should tailor it to fit your particular issues and concerns.

To that end, here are four variables that will help you determine the types of clauses and language that would work in your own post-nup:

- **Make allowances for backsliding.** In the Rosenthals' post-nup, Mindy wanted Bert to attend marital counseling. Mindy, though, knew that her husband was a busy guy and his schedule—or his mood—might cause him to miss a session. So rather than including language in the post-nup that one missed session would result in her filing for divorce, she wrote that "If Bertram's schedule prevents his attendance at a session, we will reschedule in the next ten days. If Bertram misses three sessions in one year, Mindy plans to file for divorce."

It's also wise to give credit for good long-term behavior when backsliding occurs. For instance, Terry and Sally had a post-nup that focused on his drinking problem. Though Terry had been sober for ten years, an old drinking buddy of his was in town and his buddy convinced him to join him for a beer "for old time's sake." Sally wasn't happy when Terry confessed his transgression, but she had structured the post-nup so that she would only plan to file for divorce if he fell off the wagon and got drunk. If he had a drink, then he had to admit this mistake at the next AA meeting and attend meetings daily for thirty days.

Obviously, no allowance should be made for serious breaches of the post-nup—like if Terry went on a bender. Minor transgressions, however, deserve a slap on the wrist rather than a life sentence.

- **Update the post-nup.** Things change in a marriage. The terms you set forth in your post-nup when you were in your thirties may need adjustment when you're in your forties. Perhaps you created a post-nup that was designed to prevent your spouse from micromanaging your finances; it created an agreement where you both had separate checking accounts, credit cards, and so on. Over time, however, you found that these separate accounts and cards led to unexpected problems—you became suspicious about how your partner was handling her money, and because you had no access to statements per your post-nup, tensions increased. By updating the post-nup to ameliorate these tensions—adapting this clause by mandating sharing of statements on a weekly basis—you reflect the marriage's changing realities.
- **Think through a lawyer's involvement.** As an attorney, I have a natural bias in favor of lawyers writing or at least reviewing post-nups. I think this bias, though, is justified. Partnership agreements drawn up by non-lawyer businesspeople usually are incomplete. Most of the time, these contracts leave out critical points, and these omissions cost the partners far more than a lawyer's legal fee. The same thing happens when non-lawyers draw up post-nups and fail to have them vetted by attorneys. Judges will rule the post-nup unenforceable if key legal points aren't covered or if the terms violate legal norms—e.g., that a spouse who had an affair will be denied custody or that as punishment he'll forfeit all rights to marital property.

In some states judges may be particularly leery about enforcing agreements related to spouses' conduct. A lawyer can assist in preparing a post-nup with the best chance of being accepted by a court.

As a general rule, the simpler the issues in a post-nup, the less need there is for a lawyer to write the document. Even then, though, it's smart to have an attorney review it to determine if anything is misstated or omitted that could cause problems down the road.

In addition, if you involve a lawyer, he's likely to advise you and your spouse to obtain separate legal representation; this ensures that both your interests are addressed in a post-nup. In some instances, couples are in agreement on all the issues, and they feel comfortable using only one attorney. In this case, the attorney is likely to say that he can only represent one person and that the other must sign an agreement acknowledging this fact and agreeing to it.

• **Seek fairness.** This isn't just idealistic advice, it's a practical suggestion. The more fair your post-nup is, the more likely the participants will attempt to change the behaviors that are hurting the marriage. Just as important, a fair post-nup is one that a judge is more likely to uphold. If a judge feels a post-nup is punitive, he'll throw it out. Judges want post-nups to be equitable; they want to believe that you both have discussed the agreement thoroughly, addressed each of your issues, and created terms relative to property, custody, visitation, and other matters that are reasonable.

Fairness can be a high bar to clear when you start creating the post-nup. When the catalyst for the post-nup is one spouse's bad behavior—an affair, maxing out credit cards, and so on—the victimized spouse is going to be angry. If she knows her spouse is fearful of her filing for divorce, she may be tempted to leverage that knowledge and demand behavioral changes and "reparations" that are egregious.

If you're in this position, be aware that the short-term satisfaction of holding your spouse's feet to the fire will be offset by a judge rejecting your post-nup. It's usually possible to create behavioral incentives that have a strong impact on your spouse but that are also reasonable. The key, though, is to seek fairness first and subordinate your desire to draw blood because of what your spouse has done. If you look at the three post-nups in this chapter, you'll find that they seek to address spouses' behaviors in ways that feel fair. In the Rosenthals' post-nup, Bert can no longer ask his secretary to accompany him on business trips. This is a reasonable request. Asking him to fire his secretary would not be reasonable. Bert wants Mindy to show him her cell phone weekly so he can review the calls and texts she's received—he wants to make sure that the affair with Jack McKiver is over. If, on the other hand, Bert insisted that Mindy spend no time alone or communicate with anyone of the opposite sex, that would be excessive and unfair.

Assess Your Post-Nup Type

Becoming familiar with the different ways a post-nup can be structured—and the different issues you can address and behavior-related clauses you can include—will make it much easier to discuss this topic with your spouse and figure out the post-nup that's right for both of you. Later, you'll have much more information at your disposal to put a post-nup into practice. For now, be aware of your marital issues, the different ways a post-nup may help you resolve them, and how, if it can't resolve them, it can make a divorce less financially and emotionally painful.

Think about the type of post-nup that might serve your relationship best by answering the following questions.

• **Is there a single issue that is causing problems in your relationship?** Are you or your spouse behaving in such a way that it threatens the marriage? If you had a post-nup that focused only on this issue (like the Smiths' post-nup), might you be able to create behavior-related clauses that would motivate your spouse to change his counterproductive actions?

• **Are your relationship issues varied and complex?** Do you have significant financial issues—a spouse whose spending habits are bankrupting the family—and that have ramifications on the kids' college education, maintenance and child support, retirement? Are there children/spouses from previous marriages whose relationship with your spouse is affecting your marriage negatively? Do both you and your spouse have problems with the other's behaviors; do both of your behaviors need to be addressed in order to save the marriage? Given the complexity and variety of your marital issues, might a longer, more detailed post-nup (like the one for the Jacksons) be appropriate?

• **Are you and your spouse in general agreement about the issues causing problems in your marriage?** Does your spouse hate to deal with long, legal contracts? Would he be more amenable to an agreement that was short and written in plain English? Would both of you prefer a post-nup that you wrote yourself and then brought in to an attorney to review (like the Rosenthals' post-nup)?

3

The Need for Post-Nups

Saving and Sustaining Good Marriages

WHY NOW? If post-nuptial agreements are so useful, why have they taken so long to take hold in our society? Let's start out with an essential truth: things are much more complicated than they used to be. This applies to everything from a couple's finances, to their work situations, to the way they raise their kids, to the divorce process itself. Today's couples face paradox, uncertainty, and more options than ever before as they attempt to make the right choices in their lives. People often are confused about major decisions and under great stress.

None of this is good for a marriage or, if the marriage doesn't work out, for the divorce. So the simple explanation for why post-nups are so viable today is that they help lessen the stress and confusion that threaten even good marriages. But furthermore, there are specific issues that are making post-nups so relevant to people's lives today, starting with the nature of modern marriage and divorce.

Bargaining Within an Equal Relationship

It's only relatively recently that society and the legal system presumed equality within marriages. Even thirty years ago, the presumption was that husbands would take care of wives, both financially and in other respects. A number of forces, from the debate over the Equal Rights Amendment to the feminist movement to changes in family law, have helped diminish the effects of a traditionally paternalistic society. While we still haven't achieved a pure, 50/50 ideal, much more balance exists today than in the past.

As a result, spouses are more inclined to bargain with each other now than when roles were socially codified and men had more power in relationships. Back then, there wasn't much to bargain about—the law was clear about who got what in divorces, and within marriages, men were often the breadwinners and women the housewives. Even though there were exceptions, the commonly accepted roles and legal rules dissuaded people from negotiating about their marriage.

In a more egalitarian environment, however, couples are inclined to negotiate, and that's where a post-nup proves useful. It provides a forum for debate and innovative ideas to restore balance to a marriage or make a divorce settlement fair. A woman might put in a post-nup that she will go back to school in five years to get her law degree, and that at that time her spouse has to take on a greater share of the child-raising responsibility. She might also include a provision that in the event of a divorce, he will be responsible for picking the kids up from school and other tasks that will allow her time to complete her law degree.

Today's more egalitarian roles in marriages also make it easier to talk about the issues that will be hammered out in a post-nup. While it may be less prevalent of an issue today, couples used to be less willing to confront problems and assert themselves with their partners. Typically, people were in denial that problems even existed; or they recognized that there were problems but feared that a discussion would provoke a catastrophic (for the relationship) fight. When divorce had more of a stigma, denial was used to avoid that outcome. Now, we recognize the value of open, honest, and regular communication. People are willing to confront each other and engage in conflict. When two people who love each other feel as if they can say anything and talk about any subject, they can discuss and debate everything, from childcare responsibilities to sex to what happens in the event of a divorce. They just need a nudge to get the conversation started, and the post-nup provides it.

Not only have attitudes toward equal roles in a marriage changed, but attitudes about divorce have as well. In the past, people stayed in bad marriages far longer than they should have in part because of the stigma associated with divorce. More recently, people remained in these marriages even as the stigma faded because of their fear of the cost, stress, and the possibly unfavorable decisions of the court. The post-nup helps mitigate this fear, providing a needed alternative that can decrease the cost and anxiety associated with divorce. It can also make the process more inclusive, taking some of the power out of the hands of the legal system and giving couples greater influence over the outcomes (assuming they can reach agreement in a post-nup).

From Pre-Nup to Post-Nup

As evidenced by the rise of alternative dispute resolution tactics—arbitration, mediation, counseling, etc.—the current trend is for couples to take greater responsibility in resolving their marital problems. This is most clearly evident in the growing acceptance of pre-nups by the courts. While pre-nups have been around for years, they have gained popularity as individual states have passed legislation recognizing these agreements. In Illinois, for instance, the

Uniform Premarital Agreement Act was adopted in 1989.* As soon
as a 50/50 split of marital assets became the norm, prenups became
a tactic of affluent individuals to weed out those who were only
marrying them for their money. Though prenups have received the

---

* The Uniform Premarital Agreement Act provides:

> Sec. 4. Content. (a) Parties to a premarital agreement may contract
> with respect to:
> (1) the rights and obligations of each of the parties in any of the
> property of either or both of them whenever and wherever acquired
> or located;
> (2) the right to buy, sell, use, transfer, exchange, abandon, lease,
> consume, expend, assign, create a security interest in, mortgage,
> encumber, dispose of, or otherwise manage and control property;
> (3) the disposition of property upon separation, marital dissolution,
> death, or the occurrence or nonoccurrence of any other event;
> (4) the modification or elimination of spousal support;
> (5) the making of a will, trust, or other arrangement to carry out
> the provisions of the agreement;
> (6) the ownership rights in and disposition of the death benefit
> from a life insurance policy;
> (7) the choice of law governing the construction of the agreement;
> and
> (8) any other matter, including their personal rights and obligations,
> not in violation of public policy or a statute imposing a criminal
> penalty.
> (b) The right of a child to support may not be adversely affected
> by a premarital agreement.

Although some judges may be unwilling to enforce post-nuptial conduct
clauses, the UPAA defines a much broader scope for what may be included
in a prenuptial agreement, asserting that parties to an agreement may
contract with respect to "any" matter, "including their personal rights
and obligations, not in violation of public policy or a statute imposing a
criminal penalty." The American Law Institute Principles also allow for a
broad scope.

most media publicity when they involve celebrities or other wealthy individuals, they signify a shift in legal attitude, recognizing that couples should have a greater say in all decisions that affect their marriage and divorce.

Prenups paved the way for post-nups. Once the courts recognized the validity of prenuptial agreements, it followed that the same principle applied to agreements made after people were married. In a recent divorce case in Maine involving a husband and wife who co-owned a business, for instance, the courts referred to a 2013 statute, upholding the couple's earlier agreement on alimony in the ultimate settlement. Increasingly, states are either passing similar statutes that recognize the validity of a couple's earlier agreement regarding maintenance, property division, custody, and other matters, or case law is indicating that this is the direction of court decisions on these issues.

Post-nups are becoming an accepted tool from a legal perspective. In the past, the courts rendered a decision about marital matters based on the adversarial legal process (if a settlement involving lawyers couldn't be reached). Now, there's a movement to let couples work out their own problems, whether through mediation, arbitration, or post-nups. This means that the post-nups couples create are likely to be seen as binding legal documents.

In fact, even though judges will generally adhere to state-mandated guidelines regarding custody and child support over preferences stated in a post-nup, a post-nup can be used to assist a judge in making a determination about these issues. For example, in a post-nup agreement, Jane acknowledges that she has passed out from drinking ten times in the last year; she's often unavailable when the kids come home from school and they have had to attend to their own needs upon arriving home. In the post-nup, Jane admits that she is an alcoholic and that, until she has become sober for a significant period of time, her husband, Joe, should be the custodial parent. Further, their post-nup states that, in the event of divorce, payment of 28 percent of Jane's salary at the current level far exceeds the financial need to care for their two children. Based upon expenditures over the past three years for both children, they believe that child support should be reduced by 10 percent. In addition, the post-nup includes a provision that Jane will contribute $3,000 per year to a 529 account to help pay for the kids' college expenses.

The guidance provided by this post-nup may influence the judge to deviate from standard child support payments; he'll deem the post-nup fair. As we've discussed, fairness is a critical factor to consider. For instance, when pre-nups fail to provide disclosure about a given individual's assets or when they're created in haste (e.g., on the day of the wedding), then the courts may throw them out. The same general principle applies to the creation of post-nups—they need to be seen as fair rather than one-sided or punitive. No agreement is going to be upheld by a court if it strikes the court as egregiously unfair or there's evidence that a spouse was coerced into signing it.

Assuming the post-nup is reasonable and entered into freely by both spouses—and if attorneys are involved to ensure that everything meets the legal criteria—then they should prove to be key factors in divorce decisions. This is a statement that couldn't have been made as little as five or ten years ago, but it's now one that is increasingly true in most states.

Expectations and Change

When roles are clear, when the societal status quo is maintained, when the church has a strong influence in people's lives, and when communities and cultures are stable, marriages tend to be strong. For many years in the United States as well as in other Western countries, these factors were in place. As a result, couples usually operated on the same wavelength. Shared expectations helped couples make decisions and avoid arguments. Stable finances and communities helped avoid making difficult, stress-inducing choices.

Today, everything has changed. Relationships are often destabilized by financial pressures, the need to make seemingly impossible decisions (should we move halfway across the world so one spouse can take advantage of a great professional opportunity?), and the clashing expectations common to an age of change (e.g., he expects to live near his parents, she wants to live in a more environmentally conscious community).

In this volatile reality, expectations need to be managed and communicated, and post-nups achieve these objectives. Before looking at how they do so, let's focus on the factors that make it so challenging to maintain a good marriage.

• **Dual-earning couples.** When spouses both work, a variety of conflicts arise that may seem minor initially but can become major if not addressed. Typically, conflicts occur over responsibilities for kids—who makes dinner, who cleans up after dinner, who drives them to school, who takes off when they are sick, and so on. In addition, disagreements about how to spend money are common, since both wage-earning spouses feel they should have a say in this decision. Because dual-earning spouses are a relatively recent phenomenon—many couples grew up in households where Dad worked and Mom was a housewife—there isn't a precedent to follow. Consequently, couples need to negotiate terms to resolve these conflicts before they blow up into major marital issues.

• **Changing parental responsibilities.** Today's kids don't go and spend their days fishing at the creek with their friends or playing pickup baseball at a local sandlot. Instead, they are involved in structured activities—far more than in the past. Many parents today feel pressured to attend every activity with which their kids are involved—piano recitals, Little League games, and so on. They may also feel that they should coach teams their kids are on, chaperone trips, and participate in other groups that their children belong to. In some cases, one parent takes on the lion's share of these responsibilities, creating resentment. In other instances, a running battle ensues in which parents are constantly debating who is going to attend what game on a given day. Again, many adults grew up in households where their parents rarely if ever attended their activities, and so they lack a model for how to deal with these changing circumstances. The quantity of children's activities, too, has increased. It's not unusual for a child to be taking violin lessons, going to gymnastics summer camp, and participating in Scouts or some similar group.

- **The I-want-it-now mentality.** Many couples used to scrimp and save in order to purchase homes or take vacations. They created savings plans designed to build their resources over time so they could afford to make major purchases. Now, because of the ease of credit and an inability to delay gratification, people buy homes, boats, cars, and other big-ticket items sooner rather than later. Many times, this places financial stress on the relationship. It is especially likely to create this stress when one person is a saver and the other is a spender. It's not unusual for one spouse to run up big charges on a credit card without the other spouse's knowledge—or at least without that knowledge until suddenly he or she discovers that there is a $18,000 outstanding balance on a card, creating a huge argument.

- **Accessibility of sex, drugs, and other temptations.** The Internet, mobile technology, and smartphones all make it far easier than it was in the past to indulge in addictive or counterproductive behaviors. From Internet porn to the purchase of illegal drugs to online gambling, addictive activities are only one click or call away. To err is human, but our digital world makes it all too easy to err. This creates tremendous stress on marriages, and one of the common reasons people file for divorce is because a spouse is spending hours every day online—sometimes on porn sites, sometimes in more innocuous ways (e.g., playing online games). In either instance, this spouse is ignoring his partner and the kids and sometimes spending a lot of money on this online activity.

Timely Advantages

In an age of complexity and change, we need to find a way to communicate with greater clarity and honesty in our relationships. To preserve a good marriage, people need to confront counterproductive behaviors in an effective manner as soon as they possibly can and resolve the issues they raise. It is the rare relationship today that thrives without this confrontation and resolution. If nothing is done, resentment and frustration build to the boiling point, and by then it may be too late to do anything.

Post-nups are designed to serve as this timely intervention, a way to prevent resentment and frustration. Let's look at three ways they achieve this objective:

- **Facilitating communication about key issues.** Separateness of knowledge can tear relationships apart. Joan, for instance, never knew that her husband, Bill, was racking up major charges on his credit card related to his gambling problem. She had known about the problem earlier in their marriage but she had assumed her husband now had it under control. It was only when she received a call from a collection agency about a long-unpaid bill that she got wind of what was going on. Joan was furious at Bill and was ready to divorce him the moment she found out.

Separateness of knowledge can involve all sorts of areas. One spouse may know everything about their children's schedules while the other spouse knows almost nothing. One spouse is aware of their investment strategy and tactics while the other spouse is in the dark. One spouse handles everything to do with home maintenance while the other knows little about these matters.

Sometimes, the problem is that people feel they're being kept out of the loop. Other times, they resent that their spouse shows little interest in staying informed about a key area of their lives. Post-nups can be structured so that this imbalance of knowledge is addressed. They can stipulate that all credit card charges are to be reviewed and discussed monthly or that both spouses have online access to the account. They can call for a given spouse to make a regular effort to stay informed about a child's activities. These are relatively simple actions, but once they're written out and agreed to in a formal, legally binding document, they create the accountability that helps change behaviors.

- **Reducing stress.** Much of the stress in a typical marriage is caused by low-simmering disappointments and resentments rather than knock-down, drag-out fights. In the latter, at least couples get to vent and put the issues on the table. What really grates on people, though, are the smaller things—why the husband has to travel so much for work and isn't available to attend important family functions; how the wife, since going back to work, has been frazzled by trying to balance the demands of her job with those of her family. Post-nups can delineate the behaviors that irritate spouses and provide corrective guidelines—John will limit his travel to five days per month; Joan will be able to hire a nanny to help take care of the kids when she's not around.

- **Resetting expectations.** Expectations in every marriage run the gamut—they might pertain to where the couple lives, what type of residence (condo versus house), where and how often they vacation, or the religion in which the children are raised. Change can often play havoc with a couple's expectations—what they expect both from their partners and from the marriage itself. For example: On the most basic level, Sam expects that his wife, Cindy, will stay home and take care of the children, since that is what her mother and his mother did. Perhaps they even talked about this issue early on and agreed that having Cindy stay home is best for the kids. But when Sam changed jobs, he had to take a pay cut and the bonuses haven't been great in recent years. Though they might still get by on his salary alone, it won't be easy. Therefore, Cindy has been looking for jobs, and when Sam finds out, he's livid.

Peer group pressure—say all of Cindy's friends who are moms are embarking on careers—often contributes to creating change, along with factors such as a new, prevailing social norm, financial struggles or windfalls, career moves, and so on.

Post-nups help weather these changes by clarifying expectations through forcing couples to express their views on a subject, discuss it fully, and hammer out an agreement about a given issue. When change occurs, the couple can revisit known expectations and move forward based on new and approved expectations as necessary. Perhaps Sam acknowledges the need for Cindy to work so they'll have an easier time of it financially, and perhaps Cindy compromises and takes a part-time job. Dealing with these types of issues sooner rather than later can prevent the gap between a couple's expectations from growing too wide and divisive.

Is the Marriage Really Worth Saving?

This is a valid question, given this chapter's context. Behind the question is the fear that a post-nup may be used to save a bad marriage; that a relationship that should end is prolonged because of the pressure to keep the marriage intact. Here's a modern paradox that applies: given all the forces that make it harder than ever before to sustain a marriage, there's social pressure to try and preserve relationships. Former President Obama is one of many prominent leaders who has spoken of the advantages to society of stable households and marriages. From politicians to clergy to psychologists, people are speaking out about the value of marriage, how it's a crucial institution for raising emotionally healthy children and creating strong communities. Studies even show that married men live longer than single ones.

But the validity of these perspectives is based on the marriage being healthy; post-nups should *not* be used to maintain a bad marriage. Of course, it's not always easy to know if you have a good marriage with problems or a bad marriage with some good moments. Even suggesting how to answer this question is beyond my expertise, but you should consider this issue seriously before deciding to put a post-nup to use.

Most obviously, if physical abuse is occurring, your first priority should be your physical safety and well-being. Once you are removed from any physical threats, you can consult with appropriate professionals to see if the marriage should be saved.

Less obviously, a misalignment of a couple's core values may also prove to be an irresolvable problem. Even the Catholic Church, which holds the institution of marriage to be sacred, recognizes this truth. In a Catholic marriage, when one spouse wants to have kids and the other doesn't, the church usually grants an annulment. Clearly their values are not the same, creating a fundamental flaw in the marriage. From a secular standpoint, a common value clash is over location. For instance, Gene wants to move the family to Los Angeles because he's a film director and that's where he is likely to have the most successful career. His wife, Sue, hates the idea of raising her kids in Los Angeles because of the sense of entitlement and materialism that is fostered in affluent areas of L.A.; she thinks Boston is the best place for them to live. Gene, on the other hand, isn't bothered by the prospect of raising his children in Los Angeles; he believes that they can raise good kids anywhere.

While there are possible solutions to this value clash—Gene and Sue can have a bi-coastal relationship, for instance—it's likely to create a divide in the marriage that is difficult to bridge over time. Still, a post-nup can help a couple such as Gene and Sue attempt to find a solution. They may include stipulations in a post-nup that sets out the rules for a bi-coastal relationship; or they may create childraising parameters if Sue agrees to move to L.A., such as never buying their kids cars or taking other actions that foster a sense of entitlement. Even if the post-nup can't save a marriage such as this one, at least a couple can know they've truly tried to find solutions, so they can move on without regrets and what-ifs.

Assess the Post-Nup's Potential to Save and Sustain

To help you determine if a post-nup will help you deal effectively with the issues that threaten your marriage, I've created a list of questions that will help you evaluate whether a post-nup is appropriate for you. As you'll see, these questions address the timely topics I've discussed here—changing circumstances, increasing stress, evolving expectations—that cause rifts in marriages but aren't necessarily fatal.

- **Have you recently had a shift in income?** This could be a segue from being a one-income household to two incomes. Or it could be in the opposite direction, and you have moved from two-incomes to one because of childcare issues or job loss. Has this transition created stress and arguments?
- **Have you found that your expectations about certain areas of the marriage clash with those of your spouse?** Is there conflict around where you live, how you spend or save money, or how you raise the kids? Are these conflicts more a question of circumstance (e.g., a possible job transfer) rather than core values?

- **Does your spouse exhibit addictive behaviors that you're having trouble talking about?** Do these behaviors have to do with gambling, sex, or drug addictions?

- **Is there tension or arguments about taking care of the kids?** Does one of you take on much more of this responsibility than the other? Does this create anger and resentment?

- **Have your circumstances changed since you were married?** Are you confronted by issues such as being downsized out of a job, grappling with a blended family (e.g., you had a stepchild move in with you unexpectedly), relocating away from your support network, and so on? Have these changes created marital problems that are difficult to resolve or even discuss?

If you answered yes to even some of these questions, it's likely that a post-nup can be an effective tool for your marriage. At the very least, it will bring these problematic issues out into the open and give you the opportunity to formalize potential solutions. Your "yes" answers reflect the common issues that affect many marriages in today's fast-changing, complex environment, and they're ones that the post-nup was created to deal with. Though there is no guarantee that a post-nup will save or sustain your marriage, it is a powerful tactic that increases the odds of making your relationship work over the long term.

Now let's look at a good initial step for creating a post-nup—a step that you and your partner have probably already taken even though you haven't done so in a formal manner.

4

The Marriage Contract

A Critical Preliminary Step

WHEN ASKED ABOUT THEIR MARRIAGE CONTRACTS, most couples respond with a perplexed look. They know that marriage is a legally binding relationship, but as to what the specific contract is, they usually don't have a clue. Years ago, when societal norms strongly defined gender roles, this lack of understanding had fewer negative repercussions. Back then, a husband's and wife's responsibilities within the marriage were generally well understood: the husband usually was the primary breadwinner, the wife took care of the children.

Today, much has changed, which has often led to different expectations by the spouses—one person expects X, the other person expects Y, and neither realizes that these clashing expectations exist until they surface and cause major marital problems. For instance, Jim and Joan get married and Jim assumes Joan will stop working when they have children a few years down the road. After their first child, though, Joan tells him that she intends to return to work, in large part because she makes more money at her job than he does. Jim is furious but figures that Joan will miss their child and eventually decide to be a full-time mom. In fact, after they have two more children, Joan returns to work each time, and each time more tension is added to the relationship until finally it turns into an all-out war where Jim gives Joan an ultimatum: Stay home or else!

Instead of risking the "or else," you and your spouse should make the effort to discuss and create your personal marriage contract. Ideally, this would take place before you get married, but if it did not, set aside time to go over each of your expectations at whatever point you're at in your marriage. By doing so, you facilitate the creation of a post-nup that will flow from these articulated expectations.

What Should a Marriage Contract Include?

In many ways, a marriage contract governs a husband-wife relationship in the same way that a business contract governs a long-term commercial partnership. The difference, of course, is that the former usually isn't put in writing. Instead, it's a loose understanding between spouses about major issues such as where they'll live and how many children they'll have, as well as important but smaller subjects such as careers and vacations. Many times couples think they are clear about what they signed up for, but in reality, misunderstandings and false assumptions are common.

Let's start out by examining what comprises a good marriage contract.

- **Defined roles**: as marital partner, as parent, as breadwinner, etc.
- **Codes of conduct**: what constitutes acceptable (and unacceptable) behavior, such as drinking, drugs, outside relationships, and so on.
- **Conflict resolution methods**: a mutually acceptable method of engaging in and managing disagreements.

Within these three areas, a range of topics can be addressed, from how often a couple will visit their in-laws to whether they aspire to live in a city or the suburbs to how they spend and save money. In fact, the contract can address seemingly mundane issues such as who does the chores or when to inform the other spouse if you're going to be late for dinner.

Typically, couples discuss some or even many of these issues before they're married or in the early years of the marital relationship. Unfortunately, these discussions don't always achieve consensus. Too often they're informal conversations that are poorly remembered by both parties or they are incomplete discussions that might achieve only some agreement in some areas. Still, most couples would say that they have some type of informal contract—that they've talked about some issues and that they're in general agreement on some of the points.

But this isn't enough, and these informal contracts can hamper rather than help in the creation of the post-nup. Here are the three most common problems with these types of contracts.

- The implicit assumptions about the agreement may not be shared by both spouses.
- The evolutionary nature of the relationship means what was true at the beginning is no longer true for one spouse as the marriage moves forward.
- The contract lacks legal enforceability.

To remedy these problems, you need to take steps to formalize the marriage contract, and that effort begins with thinking about your wedding vows and their implications.

Creating a Contract That Matters and Makes Sense

Whether you recited traditional vows at your wedding or created your own, they represented an exchange of promises. Typically, these promises include forsaking all others and providing unconditional love to your spouse. A typical "add-on" is a commitment to raising children in a given religious faith. Beyond that, vows can range widely, including everything from a pledge to visit faraway lands to going for walks in the woods together.

Vows alone, however, aren't sufficient to form a marriage contract. Looking back on your vows after a few or more years of marriage is an instructive exercise. You're likely to find that those vows didn't cover a wide range of issues, and that what you pledged then is not what you would pledge now.

Part of the problem with vows from a legal standpoint is that they tend toward the general, and contracts are specific. In an ad hoc way, you've probably talked about these specific issues before and during the marriage. You decide to move from the suburbs to the city; you and your spouse agree to have kids in five years; you determine where you're going to celebrate holidays (with your parents or your in-laws).

If a couple who is dating can't agree on some or many of the specifics during their talks about these subjects, then it's unlikely they'll go on to get married. Most of the time, though, some common ground exists that communicates to both people that they're on the same page in terms of lifestyle, children, and so on. In a very real sense, dating allows a couple to negotiate their initial marriage contract. They may not agree on all the clauses, but they feel like they have a lot—enough—in common.

What they may fail to do, though, is figure out a method for solving problems. In the old days, problems were often solved by gender—Dad decided about money issues, Mom decided about the kids. There was no need to discuss this part of the marriage contract, because society dictated who was responsible for what area. Now, problem-solving has become more complex and couples may marry without a clear idea of who is responsible for what issue and what they'll do when they disagree about kids, living situations, vacations, and so on.

Some couples try living together prior to marriage, and you would think this would give them a great opportunity to negotiate their marriage contract. Unfortunately, that often isn't the case. Some studies have shown that divorce rates are higher among couples who cohabited prior to marriage than among those who did not live together; others suggest that age at the time of marriage is a more important factor. Many people when living together bend over backward to compromise and accommodate the other person. After six months or a year of cohabitation, couples may become overconfident in their abilities to solve whatever problems come their way, and they are unprepared for the challenges that arise after a longer period of time and more complex issues that didn't cause problems during their cohabitation period (e.g., raising children).

As you can see, a series of obstacles stand in the way of creating a marriage contract that serves couples in good times and bad. To overcome them, it helps to think in contractual terms. In business, contracts help partners deal with conflicting assumptions and changes effectively. In personal relationships, post-nups can serve this purpose. To understand how, we first need to understand why marriage contracts, generally worthless from a legal standpoint, provide starting points for creation of post-nups.

An Unenforceable Contract

In business contracts, if one partner does not live up to his obligations to the other partner, he breaches the contract, and the other partner can take him to court to enforce the contract or, more typically, make the offending party pay the equivalent value for the loss caused by the breach.

In marriages, the most common marital breach is infidelity, and it certainly is the cause of a lot of divorces. Breaching the marital contract by committing an infidelity, however, does not carry with it a clearly agreed-upon approach that is aimed at saving the marriage or achieving a reasonable marital settlement agreement in the event of a repeat of the problem. While divorce is usually a disincentive for future similar conduct, when one spouse gives the other a second chance, a post-nup makes the cheating spouse think twice about doing so again. Essentially, a post-nup provides the marital contract with teeth.

More than that, it also helps clarify implicit assumptions and deal with misrepresentations. For instance, one spouse may assume that it's fine to continue to accept financial support from his parents after the marriage, while the other spouse assumes this support would end as soon as they were wed. When she discovers that they are still financially dependent on his parents, an argument ensues that becomes a recurring one in the marriage: She says this financial support creates a psychological dependence on his parents. He counters that they have plenty of money and it makes their lives easier, so why not accept it. If unresolved, this argument can grow and widen and threaten the marriage.

Post-nups force couples to openly communicate about issues like this and forge mutually acceptable resolutions. It may be that the husband agrees to cut off all financial support from his parents by a certain date, or that they agree to pay the parents back some of the money they've been given. Whatever the resolution, it takes a potentially devastating issue (to the marriage) off the table. By dealing with this issue as business partners would within a contractual context, couples help defuse a potential powder keg.

Sometimes, people make bad assumptions because of their spouses' misrepresentations. In certain cases, these misrepresentations are relatively minor—one person denies he was ever involved roman- tically with a woman they both know, for instance. In other cases, these misrepresentations are more serious—hiding a gambling debt or not telling a spouse about a child from a former marriage. Post-nups can't do much about a truly devious spouse. If someone is marrying you for your money and pretends to be in love, a post-nup discussion is unlikely to reveal this truth (though it can afford you some protection when you divorce). What the post-nup discussion can do, however, is give you and your spouse the opportunity to come clean about a troubling issue from your past. Sooner or later, most misrepresentations are exposed through behaviors. You're hiding a gambling debt from the past and you start gambling again after you've been married; or your ex-husband, who you failed to mention to your current husband, shows up at your door. When behaviors reveal misrep- resentations, they can destroy marriages. People rightly feel hurt when they have been deceived, and they have trouble regaining trust in their spouse.

Ideally, post-nups will provide conversational forums for spouses to clear the air about their past. Realistically, however, they may also serve as tools to help spouses negotiate the consequences of future potential misrepresentations. When Sally discovers that Jerry has hidden a past substance abuse problem and it resurfaces four years into their marriage, she confronts him and they set up a post-nup that incentivizes him to attend drug rehab and not to use drugs again at any point in the future. Because the post-nup puts legal muscle into the marriage contract, it often can deal with misrepresentation effectively.

Negative Consequences as Well as Forgiveness

Most of us would like to believe that if our spouse breaches the marriage contract in some way—infidelity, alcohol or drug abuse, gambling, and so on—that it's only a one-time problem; that with conversation, counseling, and forgiveness, the breaching spouse will have learned his lesson and won't make the same mistake twice.

Unfortunately, people may repeat their bad behaviors if there's no specific, pre-negotiated negative consequence for doing so. It's not that I have a pessimistic view of how couples behave within a marriage, but rather that I understand that good, loving people can do bad things. People rationalize their bad behaviors, and there may even be some truth in their rationalizations. In business, for instance, one partner may find a way to take a larger piece of compensation than is his due based on his rationalization that "I did more of the work and brought in more of the customers than my partner." With a contract in place that provides serious penalties for taking compensation above and beyond the sum that is stipulated, however, this partner will be much less likely to make this mistake.

To put it more bluntly, people need to be reminded that actions have consequences. They can't be allowed to rationalize their behaviors and think they're entitled to the bad behavior in which they indulge. Consider that when people forgive their spouses for having an affair, they hope that their willingness to forgive will give the marriage a fresh start. Typically, the cheating spouse, after a big blowup, promises he'll remain faithful. In fact, this individual may have taken the lack of consequences for his breaking the marriage contract as a sign that he is free to violate it again.

In an ideal world, of course, there would be no need for these negative sanctions. In business too, the phrase "my handshake is my bond" should be universally accepted. In our complex and volatile world, however, contracts serve a valuable purpose. People need to be reminded that if they are guilty of egregious behavior, they will suffer the consequences. For the majority of couples, post-nups will serve more as deterrents than punishments. Spouses will recognize that their marriage contract carries legal weight in the event of a divorce, and they will think twice before they behave in ways that violate that contract because the essential terms of a divorce have been set forth in the post-nup.

All of us need these reminders upon occasion. It's why speed limits are posted and why people are given tickets if they exceed these limits. Post-nups remind spouses about what's important in marriage and in life, and they help them think before they act.

Renegotiating the Contract

Many business contracts are examined and revised periodically. Annual performance reviews are required by many companies. These reviews in the business world are based on the knowledge that situations change. Say a senior partner wants to sell off part of the company to his junior partner, or titles shift and so responsibilities need to be reassigned. The recognition exists that for the contract to remain viable, it must be reviewed regularly and changed to reflect new circumstances.

Therefore, your marriage contract not only needs to be put in writing and include penalties for violating the terms of the contract, it also has to be updated annually (or sooner, if there is an obvious change). This isn't always easy to do, since discussions about the marriage contract can involve difficult subjects. You may feel like you had to work hard to convince your spouse to discuss this contract in the first place and hammer out an agreement, and that you shouldn't have to do it all over again.

Unfortunately, relationships are even more evolutionary than businesses, and if you don't update the contracts that govern them when needed, you may be stuck with a contract that no longer addresses the issues that are paramount in your life. Reviewing and revising contracts can be facilitated if you're aware of the issues and events that require contracts be updated. To that end, here is a list of some common life changes that may require couples to revise their marriage contracts.

- **Birth of a child.** The marriage contract should cover custody, visitation, and maintenance in the event of a divorce.

- **Career shift.** One spouse may start a new job or career, or go from working to being stay-at-home parent, or rejoin the workforce after staying home with the kids. One spouse may be a business executive who returns to work after a pregnancy, and initiates the conversation: "Now that I'm back working sixty-hour weeks, you need to take X amount of childcare duties." The post-nup contract should address how this change will affect day-to-day responsibilities in the event that a divorce settlement is the result.

- **Financial setback or windfall.** For instance, you may suffer a serious monetary loss because of a bad investment or medical expenses, or you or your spouse could inherit a significant sum of money. You need to update your contract to reflect this new financial circumstance. It may be that you can no longer afford to have one spouse stay home with the children. It may also be that if you get divorced, you no longer need to sell the house and split the proceeds.

- **Discovery of bad spousal behavior.** Your previous marriage contract didn't cover this behavior, either because it didn't exist in the past or you didn't know about it. When you discover that your spouse has a gambling problem, you need to update the contract so that it includes a clause that requires him to take certain steps to manage or end this behavior.

Assess Your Marriage Contract

Thinking about your marriage contract will facilitate creation of your post-nup. When people first hear about post-nuptial agreements, they often aren't sure what belongs in them or they are overwhelmed by all the issues they think they should address in this legal document. When people think and talk about the marriage contract first, it helps them identify the key points that matter to them in their marriage. These points are often the foundation of the post-nup.

To help you consider your marriage contract, look at the following questions and discuss them with your spouse.

- **What were your wedding vows?** Did you merely recite the standard vows or did you and your spouse write your own? If you created your own, do you feel that you've both upheld these vows?
- **What are the issues that you fear might hurt or destroy the contract?** If you were to assess your marriage contract as if it were a binding legal agreement, what key points would you include to increase the odds that the relationship remains viable?
- **What has changed from the start of your relationship to now?** Do you feel that at the beginning of the relationship, you and your spouse were on the same page about the marriage but that circumstances have changed how you view it? Have you ever renegotiated the contract with your spouse— talked about changes involving money, careers, and children and attempted to find and formalize a new common ground on these issues?

- **How have your spouse's behaviors violated what you perceived as the marriage contract?** Were his offending behaviors major (drinking, drugs, infidelity, gambling) or minor (refusal to participate on some family outings, insistence on living in a condo when you want to live in a house)? What negative sanctions would you include in a contract to punish him for major offending behaviors?

5

The Action Pact

How to Stop Your Spouse
(and Yourself) from Behaving Badly

A S THE NAME IMPLIES, the Action Pact is the part of the post-nup that attaches consequences to bad behavior. You may have told your spouse a thousand times to stop favoring his kids from a previous marriage over your own or that he's got to stop skipping family events to watch sports. But even if your spouse resolves to behave better, his resolve may weaken. The Action Pact strengthens that resolve by making sure continued bad conduct is addressed and terms of a divorce are agreed to while the parties seek to reconcile.

These consequences revolve around divorce—it's the best leverage one spouse has to convince the other to behave. As we'll see, these Action Pacts vary widely, reflecting the variation in bad marital behaviors. What they share in common are terms that motivate both couples to try to make the marriage work.

Action Pact Examples

To get a better sense of how Action Pact clauses function within post-nups, here are two examples of different types of behavior-related agreements. The first one involves June, who was represented by Lynn Weisberg, an attorney with my firm. June and Greg were married for fourteen years and had a ten-year-old child. June was a well-paid professional while Greg earned less and had been out of work for a while. June caught him having an affair, and as furious as she was at Greg for cheating on her, she still hoped this was a one-time thing and that they might save the marriage.

Lynn recommended a post-nup, and she and June began to create one. In the Action Pact section, June laid out the terms: no more affairs, and Greg must attend regular couples and individual counseling sessions. Just as important, June insisted that the Action Pact address her husband's financial behaviors, a concern throughout their marriage. She wanted to make sure she and her child were protected in case of a divorce, and so she created additional terms: Greg would give up any claim to their residence or her retirement plan monies (he had his own retirement savings from an earlier job). He also agreed to a split of other marital property that June deemed equitable, given her much more significant earning capacity over the course of the marriage.

Greg signed the post-nup immediately without requesting any changes. According to June, he felt guilty about his behavior and wanted to save the marriage. She added that Greg also recognized that the financial terms were fair given her superior earning power.

For a number of months, Greg adhered to the terms of the post-nup, attending counseling sessions and not having contact with the woman with whom he had the affair. But after a while, Greg decided he couldn't handle the counseling sessions anymore and refused to discuss the affair either in a therapeutic session or outside of it. This violated the terms of the Action Pact, and June filed for divorce.

With hindsight, June talks about the value of the Action Pact in ways that go beyond the immediate goal of trying to save the marriage.

"It was a critical tool for me, a godsend," she said. "The post-nup meant I did everything I could to save the marriage. Even though it didn't save it, I would have always wondered if I made the right decision [to divorce Greg immediately] if I hadn't created the post-nup and given us a second chance.

"In addition, the post-nup streamlined the divorce process. Because of our agreement, the financials had already been sorted out. This allowed us to focus on the custody issues (which weren't addressed in the post-nup) rather than be distracted by all the wrangling over money and property, and this helped us arrive at a good custody settlement."

While the most egregious problems in marriages are often affairs, addictions, and the like, all sorts of other behaviors and attitudes can threaten relationships. Post-nups can accommodate all sorts of issues, as the following example illustrates.

Martin and Aaeesha have been married for fifteen years and have four children; Martin is Catholic and Aaeesha is a Muslim. After they married and decided to have kids, they agreed that they would raise their children in both religious traditions. Though they adhered to this agreement for a while, Martin started proselytizing to the children. He placed religious statues throughout the house, played Christmas music on the whole house system for most of December, and tried to convince his children that his religion was far superior to Aaeesha's. Aaeesha was angry with her husband, and though she asked and then insisted that he stop this behavior, he refused. It was only when the situation reached a crisis point—Aaeesha told him that she was considering consulting a divorce attorney—that he was willing to engage in a conversation about how he might change his behaviors. As a result of the conversation, he and Aaeesha created a post-nup in which they agreed to very specific behavior changes—removing the religious statues from the house, only playing the religious music on Christmas, refraining from promoting his religion at the expense of his wife's. Though Martin was reluctant to make these changes, when he understood his marriage depended on it, he agreed to them in the post-nup's Action Pact.

The Theory Behind the Action Pact

The Action Pact isn't designed to work miracles—to turn a lazy, good-for-nothing bum into a saint. When I talk about behavioral change, I'm not talking about radical swings in personality. Instead, I'm referring to modest but meaningful shifts in how a given individual lives his life. It's unreasonable to expect someone who has always been shy to become the life of the party; it is reasonable to expect this introverted individual to make an effort to be social at a company party in order to make his spouse happy. Perhaps more to the point, it's reasonable to expect someone to focus attention on specific, negative behaviors that are alienating his spouse—drinking, excessive spending, etc.—and stop or mitigate them.

In fact, the theory behind the Action Pact is that in many instances, it repairs and renews the relationship rather than creates something new. Rather than asking people to take on traits and ways of interacting that are foreign to them, the pact motivates people to return to an earlier, better time in the relationship. During the early years of their relationship, a couple got along well—well enough that they committed to a permanent relationship.

Then something changed. A couple had children; they moved to a new city; one person lost his job or is struggling in a new job. Whatever the event was, it created new stress on the relationship. In response to this stress, one person begins behaving badly—spending a lot of time away from home, drinking to excess, having an affair, running up credit card debt.

The goal of the Action Pact, then, is to bring the relationship back to the way things were—or at least to a new normal that is as happy as things were during the best of times. Sometimes Action Pacts achieve this goal by addressing behaviors that are difficult to discuss, let alone change.

As I've noted, courts often have problems with determining fault—or even violations of agreements between the spouses—because most states are no-fault divorce states. That is why we are not advocating post-nups with explicit contractual triggers based upon conduct. Our solution is to have Action Pacts that address problems. If either spouse decides that the Action Pact has failed or simply has given up on the marriage (without doing what the Action Pact suggests) then the terms of divorce will apply. The judge need not determine whether a party's conduct violated the Action Pact.

When issues head into the bedroom, courts often don't follow. The more sensitive the topic, the less likely courts will insert themselves as solutions. Courts also aren't interested in examining details that, while important to the couple, may seem less important to third parties—whether one spouse gains weight, shaves every day, or employs a sex toy.

Just because courts are unlikely to address the parties' conduct does not mean that a post-nup fails as a solution. What is does mean is that, when a post-nup addresses intimate relations, it should be clear that the judge need not examine those relations—the judge merely needs to examine the terms agreed upon if a divorce ensues.

The following example with Sue and Gary shows the value of a post-nup even in situations in which a judge may refuse to consider the parties' actions or agreed-upon solutions.

Sue and Gary has been married for nineteen years, had two adolescent children, and were both employed in high-stress professional jobs. For the first fifteen years of the marriage, Sue and Gary had gotten along well and had an active sex life. But over the last four years, Gary had gradually withdrawn from physical intimacy. At first Sue chalked up his diminishing interest as a result of working long hours and dealing with a new boss—he fell asleep exhausted almost immediately every night—but then she discovered that he was visiting Internet porn sites frequently.

At first, she didn't confront him about this behavior, hoping that it would pass. But it didn't, and she struggled with how to deal with it. She was seeing a therapist and confessed her problem, explaining that she was only forty-three years old and felt rejected by her husband. Sue said she still loved him, but she felt that she had lost emotional as well as physical intimacy, and she didn't want to continue the marriage if it couldn't be restored.

The therapist suggested doing a post-nup. Sue and Gary had a series of discussions that were difficult but revealing; Gary denied visiting porn sites at first but eventually admitted he did use them, claiming that he needed "variety" and that the sites were a harmless way to get that. He also complained that Sue had gained weight; she countered that so had he. Eventually, they created an Action Pact with behavioral clauses for both of them. Gary was prohibited from visiting the porn sites, and Sue was allowed to check his various digital devices at any time to monitor whether he was keeping up his end of the bargain. Each spouse's behavior clause called for resuming regular health club workouts and making an effort to lose some weight. In addition, they both agreed to work with a sex therapist to restore their physical relationship. The Action Pact called for quarterly "reviews" of the progress they were making. During these discussions, if either Sue or Gary concluded that they weren't making progress, then they would file for divorce—an outcome both of them wanted to avoid.

Action Pacts don't always work, but they do always communicate how serious a person is about the need for a partner to change her behavior. Without an Action Pact, it's likely that Gary and Sue would have reached the point of no return. Sue would have become so frustrated with Gary's behaviors (especially the porn site use) that her ire would have built and built until she blew up at him, leaving both of them hurt and frustrated. Even if they had tried to salvage the marriage after that, that blow-up would hang over every subsequent discussion on the subject.

Ultimately, Action Pacts ask couples to do everything possible to save the marriage and be creative and open about what actions might do the trick. As you'll see, the best Action Pacts capitalize on the nature of human behavior—they take advantage of psychology.

The Psychology Behind the Action Pact

Post-nups work for many reasons. First, they foster better communication and behavior. But they also possess a powerful psychological component in the Action Pact. When you and your spouse agree to adopt certain behaviors and curtail others, you're creating marital accountability for what you say and do. Too often, people's commitment to a marriage is vague. As fervently as they may recite their marriage vows, they are likely to violate them in small and large ways at some point in the relationship. Psychologists use a term, *habituation*, that essentially means that partners grow accustomed to each other over time and what seemed fresh and exciting gradually becomes something they take for granted. Habituation loosens the bonds of commitment in a relationship and opens the door for negative behaviors.

Mark Moller-Gunderson is a retired Lutheran pastor in Lake Geneva, Wisconsin, and for years he worked with couples in his congregation who experienced marital problems. He notes that in some struggling relationships, love has disappeared from the marriage. In these cases, nothing much will help fix a couple's problems. On the other hand, Pastor Mark says, when couples are what he calls "love stubborn"—bullheaded in their commitment to loving each other— then problems have the potential to be solved.

"When people are stubborn in love, they will fight to save the marriage, and a post-nup is a tool that can help activate that stubbornness, reminding people about what's really important in their relationship," he says.

Judy Callans, a Northfield, Illinois, licensed clinical social worker who has worked with couples for twenty-eight years, related a story about a marriage going through a rough patch and how the couple created an Action Pact around a single behavior that was threatening the relationship.

Tanya was a lingerie model who was married to an abusive older man. He was a master manipulator, and he convinced Tanya to be an actress in soft-core pornographic movies and pocketed all the money she made. It was a horrible relationship, but Tanya had grown up in an abusive environment and lacked the perspective to recognize abuse when it came to relationships. She came to recognize that she was being abused, though, over the ten years of their marriage, and she filed for divorce at age thirty. Subsequently, she met Jack, a considerable improvement over her former husband, and she and Jack married. For the first few years, things went well, but Jack started bringing up Tanya's past. She had been honest with him about her past and that she was a lingerie model and appeared in X-rated movies. Now whenever Tanya blamed Jack for something, he would bring up her past, as if he wanted to show her that she isn't blameless. At first, Tanya was irritated by this behavior but soon it became more than an irritant. Though Tanya tried to explain why these references were so hurtful and Jack agreed that he would stop doing it, he still brought up her past when they had arguments.

Judy explained that except for these incidents, Jack and Tanya seem to have a good relationship and a marriage worth trying to save. While initial therapy sessions with both of them were useful and helped them understand each other's issues, Jack still reverted to his old behavior when he was under stress—i.e., when Tanya was mad at him about something he had done and they had a heated verbal argument. Judy suggested they create an agreement—a post-nup—that would incentivize Jack to find another way to deal with his frustration when Tanya was mad at him. They structured their agreement so that it has a "three strikes and you're out" Action Pact. The first two times he brings up her past, he is given a warning. The third time, Tanya will file for divorce, and as part of that divorce, he agrees that they will sell their condo and she will receive 60 percent of the proceeds.

So far, Jack is abiding by the terms of their post-nup and hasn't had a single warning.

From a psychological standpoint, post-nups seem to be a more powerful deterrent to bad behavior after a couple has at least a few years of marriage under their belts. Pastor Mark makes the point that younger couples sometimes have an idealized view of marriage and aren't realistic about what it will take to make the relationship work long term—that love isn't enough and that sometimes compromises and changes need to be made. For this reason alone, post-nups are often more effective than prenups, since couples have gained the knowledge and maturity necessary to hammer out an Action Pact and make a sincere attempt to adhere to it.

Action Pacts also foster empowerment. Judy told the story of Tim and Carrie, who had been married for fifteen years and had two kids. In many ways, it was a good marriage—Tim was a well-known business leader who served on many boards and did a lot of pro bono work for good causes, and Carrie was a great mom with lots of friends who was involved in philanthropic efforts. The problem was that Tim had a drinking problem, one that got worse over the course of their marriage. The drinking in turn led him to have an affair with another heavy drinker—a teacher at their son's school.

Though Tim and Carrie went through marriage counseling and Tim promised Carrie that the affair was over and that he would cut back on his drinking, he did not uphold those promises and Carrie could no longer believe him. It was only when they decided to do a post-nup that Tim began changing his behavior and Carrie began to feel like she had some control over the relationship. The post-nup dictated that Tim had to stop drinking and enroll in a substance abuse program; that if he refused to go to the program or dropped out, he would have to go to the well-known Hazelden Clinic in Minneapolis for treatment. Further, he had to agree that he and Carrie would call the teacher with whom he had the affair and tell her together that it was over. If Tim failed to abide by these terms, Carrie would be free to disclose his behavior to others—an outcome that Tim didn't want because he was a public figure. Also, Carrie would receive a generous settlement if a divorce happened.

All this empowered Carrie. It balanced out control in the relationship and made Carrie feel like she was on equal ground with Tim. And perhaps most significant of all, the Action Pact created a sense of accountability for both of them.

Judy explained that "when people come to therapy, they like to tell their stories. Having a witness to their story is important. But a post-nup is an official witness. It's a legal document, so that they, myself, and a lawyer know what they've agreed to do. There's a lot of he-said, she-said in therapy. Post-nups get past that and put people on the same page."

The Intensely Personalized Perception of Bad Behavior

When you think about it, you can come up with a quick list of behaviors that destroy marriages: infidelity, drinking, drugs, gambling, money problems, blended families, unemployment. But you should also recognize that the specific behavior that may end *your* marriage is significantly different from that of another couple with the same behavioral category problem. Similarly, the changes requested may be acceptable for one person and unacceptable for another. For this reason, Action Pacts need to be very specific in their language and tailored to the problems and personalities of both spouses.

Consider two marriages, both of which are threatened because of money problems. In one marriage, Andrew is spending tons of money on luxury items the family can't afford—boats, cars, televisions—as well as showering his spouse and his kids with gifts. His spouse fears that Andrew is doing this out of a deep sense of guilt—he had an affair a few years ago and it almost destroyed the marriage. He came to his senses and ended the affair, but he has been wracked with guilt ever since.

In the other marriage, Gloria also is spending a lot of money, but her spending takes the form of day trading. She's good at it and until last year had made a lot of money doing it, but her spouse worries that she's now taking too much risk. Last year, they almost had to declare bankruptcy because of a big loss Gloria incurred. Her spouse knows Gloria has a goal for her investing—she wants to be able to pay for all four kids' college educations at schools of their choosing—but he fears they won't be able to pay for any of those educations if she has another major loss.

So the same category problem results in very different Action Pacts. Andrew's Action Pact has to involve therapy that helps him deal with his guilt. Unless he finds a meaningful way to address it, he will continue to spend money the family doesn't have.

Gloria's Action Pact requires specific limits on her investing—stop limits when she reaches a specific loss point. It also requires allowing her spouse to monitor her investing daily to ensure she adheres to these limits.

With the need for tailoring Action Pacts to specific behaviors in mind, let's look at how to create these pacts.

How to Create an Effective Action Pact

As important as it is to have a lawyer help you create the post-nup, you should be able to lay the pact's foundation on your own. You know yourself and your partner—and more important, the behavior that is threatening the marriage—better than anyone else. You can use this knowledge to craft an effective Action Pact—one that (with a lawyer's assistance) should hold up in court and, ideally, help you avoid court and get the marriage back on solid ground.

Let's start out with a four-step process for putting together an Action Pact.

#1. Identify the behavior at issue. This may seem like a simple thing—e.g., "he drinks too much" or "she is spending all our money"—but specificity is crucial. Ask yourself:

- What is it specifically that your spouse has done that you can no longer tolerate?

- How long has this behavior been going on?
- Is there a level of this behavior that you're willing to tolerate? What level is unacceptable?
- What specific problems is this behavior causing you and how is it harming your marriage (e.g., stress, financial difficulties, etc.)?

Answering these questions will help you create the right language for the Action Pact, enabling you to be precise about the behavior that will trigger a divorce and the resulting consequences if this behavior isn't changed.

Be aware, too, that the Action Pact can include more than one behavior. It's possible that your spouse expects you to change a behavior—he believes that you're doing something that causes him to behave the way he does. While you don't want to "stuff" the Action Pact with an unwieldy number of behavior triggers—there's a limit to what people are capable of handling—it's fine to include more than one behavior trigger.

#2. State the promise that your spouse makes to stop or moderate the stated behavior.

- What actions must your spouse take to sustain the marriage?
- Is there one specific action or a series of actions (e.g., stopping drinking or reducing the amount consumed to an acceptable level over time) that must be taken?
- Is the goal to stop a behavior or to moderate/manage it?
- Are you willing to be held to the same promise? Some lawyers recommend that both spouses be held to the same standard (e.g., neither spouse will commit an infidelity).

#3. Specify what constitutes a violation of the promise.

- Do you insist on a zero tolerance policy (one drink and the marriage is over)?
- Can you define the latitude you're willing to grant your spouse regarding the behavior? Are you willing to tolerate one minor slip-up? What lines cannot be crossed?

#4. Lay out the consequences for breaking the promise.

- If your spouse violates the promise, how will this violation affect custody, visitation, maintenance, and other terms of the divorce? (Consult with an attorney to determine what will be seen as acceptable by the courts.)
- Given this violation, what other non-divorce repercussions do you want to see enacted (for instance, your spouse has to live outside your residence until he completes anger management therapy)?

Beyond these four steps, you can increase the odds that your Action Pact will be legally viable and a good, marriage-sustaining tool if you answer the following questions as you create the pact.

- **Is what you're asking your spouse to do realistic?** Sometimes, people demand behavioral changes in marriages that are more ideal than real. You can't expect 180 degrees of change or overnight results—hot-tempered people won't become serene overnight, and addictive personalities need time, patience, and outside support to manage their addictions. Be aware, too, that some people become so angry at their spouses because of their behaviors that they are tempted to use the Action Pact punitively. For example, they demand that their spouses quit jobs they love because they are spending too much time in the office, or they insist that husbands who cheated on them never spend a second alone with other women. Even if their spouses try to adhere to these requirements, they will probably grow to resent them since the requirements are unrealistic.

Therefore, analyze what your spouse is capable of doing. Can she stop drinking or using drugs or gambling immediately, or does she need to manage these behaviors with the supervision and support available in an ongoing program? Can he manage to curtail his excess spending according to an agreed budget, or does he need to be put on a strict allowance and run all purchasing through his spouse? Ask yourself—and ask your spouse—what you can do to help achieve the goal of the Action Pact. It may be that she needs to feel she can talk to you when she's vulnerable to falling back into old patterns, or that you won't constantly bring up his issues outside of private settings and embarrass him in front of the kids. Whatever support your spouse needs, you can build into the post-nup.

• **Is your language clear and specific?** Ambiguous and general terms defeat the purpose of an Action Pact. If the pact states that your spouse has to be "nicer" or that he must learn to make your family his number-one priority, it's difficult to translate this language into measurable actions. On the other hand, if the pact stipulates that over the next year, he must schedule twenty-four date nights with you and that he must spend three out of four weekends doing things with the family, then it's relatively easy to determine if he's fulfilling the pact.

• **Are you reviewing the pact regularly and adapting it to changes in your marriage?** As I've noted earlier, the more current post-nups are, the better. This is especially true for Action Pacts because they are focused on behaviors at specific moments in time.

To make sure Action Pacts remain current, do the following.

• **Include time limits that reward your spouse** for taking positive steps toward behavioral goals. If your spouse is an alcoholic, for instance, the pact may stipulate that if he doesn't have a drink within a year after the post-nup is signed, then he only has to attend half as many Alcoholics Anonymous meetings the following year. In this way, the pact motivates your spouse to adhere to the agreement by giving him this benefit and recognizes how his behavior has changed over time.

• **Include a review clause in the Action Pact.** This clause would state that you and your spouse will review and discuss the pact every six months or whatever time frame you deem appropriate to make sure the pact's language is still relevant to your situation. If something has changed, then you agree to revise the pact accordingly.

• **Ensure that the pact is sufficiently motivating.** The most effective Action Pacts motivate people to do better. The prospect of a divorce and other negative consequences are powerful incentives for change. While it's fine to include a range of consequences from minor (moving out of the house for a week) to major (reduced visitation based upon admission of actions that a judge would determine not to be in the best interests of the children), the key is that they're chosen with your spouse in mind. What consequence is particularly tailored to her? What negative sanction will raise his awareness of how he's acting and compel him to try to do what you request?

However, you should not only rely on negative sanctions; include *positive* ones as well. Specifically, consider including a "sunset clause" in the Action Pact. This clause is akin to probation, in that if your spouse is able to maintain the good behavior that you request for a period of time—such as a year or two—then the negative sanction associated with that behavior disappears. For instance, he doesn't have an affair for two years, and given his good behavior, the clause that stipulates that he will be denied joint custody in the event of a divorce goes away.

Sunset clauses provide powerful and positive motivation to behave in ways that a spouse requests. They function much like a juvenile court judge I knew in a rough suburb of Chicago. The judge was a huge, looming presence, and when teenagers would appear in his courtroom on some relatively minor charge, he'd say something to the effect of, "Look here, I'm going to schedule this case for a year from now. If you clean up your act and stay out of trouble for that period of time, I'll dismiss the case. But if you show up before then on another charge during that time, you're going to jail for six months and I'm going to write that down on your record right now!" As you might expect, this "agreement" was highly successful in motivating juveniles to stay out of trouble.

Targeting Marriage Contract Violations

Some Action Pacts don't include a behavior clause of the type I've just discussed because a single behavior isn't what's threatening the marriage. Instead, the problem is less well-defined—too much arguing, for instance, or one person is emotionally distant or keeps putting off important discussions about key marital issues. In other words, the implicit marriage contract is in dispute—one or both spouses' expectations of the marriage aren't being met. In these instances, the Action Pact can be used to call a halt to unproductive marital behavior, to demand the couple use a specific method to reach solutions, or to set the limits on compromise (when one spouse is always compromising to appease his or her partner, setting limits creates a more equitable relationship).

When the Action Pact is used in this way, it's similar to the behavioral counseling technique marriage counselors employ. Typically, couples make reciprocal promises to each other: "I will try to be less of a nag"; "And I will try to remember to pick up after myself." I'm simplifying this technique here, but the key is reciprocity that facilitates communication and problem-solving. Though I'm not an expert in behavioral counseling, I know that many therapists who work with couples find this approach to be effective. For instance, let's say John has promised his wife, Louise, that he'll take on more child-raising responsibilities, such as getting the kids dressed for school. If John breaks this promise, the Action Pact can stipulate that failure to help the kids get ready for school twice in one week will result in the forfeiture of his Sunday sports-watching activity. Obviously, this consequence isn't as serious as the divorce-related ones we previously discussed, but it still carries more weight than one made as part of behavioral counseling because there's a clear cause-and-effect consequence codified in a legal document.

The Action Pact can prevent problems from escalating from bad to worse. It may be that regular arguments about how the couple will spend the weekend or when they have a date night are not a threat to the marriage in the present, but they can escalate if they're not addressed. The Action Pact increases the odds that they'll be addressed effectively.

Assess Your Action Pact

This may be your biggest challenge when creating an Action Pact: Setting the behavior target so that your spouse has a good chance of hitting it. The following questions are designed to help you do a reality check of the trigger behavior and associated consequences you want to include in the Action Pact.

- **Knowing your spouse as well as you do, is she capable of taking the actions you propose?** Would you say the odds of her taking these new actions are good, average, or poor? If you answered average or poor, are there terms of the agreementyou might be willing to change to increase the odds of her doing what you request? Would it help if you included a clause that you would support her efforts to change in some way? Would it help if you made seeing a counselor/therapist a mandatory part of the agreement, either for her or for both of you?
- **Does the Action Pact make your spouse more accountable for his behaviors?** Does it empower him to change, and does it foster a sense of empowerment in you?
- **Do you feel the time frame for adopting a new behavior is realistic?** Would she be better able to adopt this behavior if you gave her additional months, or even years, to do as you request? Would it be better to break the changes into increments—to set weekly or monthly goals for your spouse?
- **Would those who know your spouse best feel that he is capable of adjusting his behaviors as you've outlined?** If you were to show your Action Pact to close friends or siblings, what changes (if any) would they make in the Action Pact?
- **Do you feel that the consequences are fair?** How do you think your spouse will react to the consequences attached to the failure to adopt the behaviors you've specified—will she be outraged and refuse to talk about them, be upset initially and then be open to negotiation, or will she find them acceptable? Given what you know about divorce law, will the consequences be acceptable to a judge (this is a question your lawyer should help you answer)?

6

The Property Pact

Dividing Stuff When the House
Is Not Yet Divided

THE ACTION PACT is designed to help couples save their marriage; the Property and Custody Pacts are agreements about what
will happen if the marriage can't be saved. While it might seem odd
to quote twice-divorced Donald Trump about this subject, he once
made a wise comment about prenuptial agreements: "It's a lot easier
to get done when you love each other than when you hate each other."

As you are probably aware, arguments over the house, the bank
account, visitation, and custody can become time-consuming, mon-
ey-draining, stress-inducing battles. Despite judges' efforts to render
fair decisions, these issues can become so complex that even Solomon
himself might not rule justly. In many instances, couples are in the
best position to decide who should get what, doing right by each
other and for the children.

The catch, of course, is that they're able to make the right decisions when they still care about each other and hope the marriage
can be saved. Later, they may lose all perspective.

In the next chapter, we'll examine the Custody Pact. Here the focus is to help you craft a fair and effective Property Pact as part of your post-nup.

Consequences and Fairness

The ability of a post-nup to change behavior and save a marriage is directly proportional to the consequences it sets for failing to do so. Loss of property is a very meaningful consequence. As I've emphasized throughout, post-nups allow you to make a divorce consequence-specific and meaningful. People are adept at rationalizing their behaviors and living in denial about the consequences of their actions. A post-nup that spells out exactly what will be lost if a divorce ensues is a powerful reality check.

John Winn, an attorney in New York who has created post-nups for clients, handled the post-nup involved in the divorce case of Giovanna Garner versus Andrew Garner. Their post-nup was precipitated by Andrew having an affair, and he agreed in the post-nup to give up his rights to the marital property if he were to have another affair and they were to divorce. He did, and Giovanna filed. The courts upheld the post-nup, and Winn said one of the great things about post-nups is that they allow people to do something different—and arguably, more fair—than what a state's statutes dictate.

Property clauses like this have been ruled valid in a number of states and the trend is moving toward enforcement. It is only in the last six years that the Supreme Court of Connecticut first approved of post-nups involving Property Pacts, and New Hampshire did the same only four years ago. The Connecticut Supreme Court held that "[p]ostnuptial agreements are consistent with public policy" because they "realistically acknowledge the high incidence of divorce" and "allow two mature adults to handle their own financial affairs." New Hampshire's Supreme Court stated, "The modern view is that spouses may freely enter contractual relationships, and courts will uphold them if they satisfy the criteria of contract formation and are otherwise fair." A Kansas court approved post-nups involving Property Pacts in 2012 and a Massachusetts court did the same in 2010. In Pennsylvania, for instance, Robert and Barbara Laudig created a post-nup after Barbara had an affair. They went through a separation, a time when Barbara moved out of their home. She moved back, however, when they reconciled—a reconciliation fostered by the creation of a post-nup. The post-nup stated that if Barbara engaged in sexual intercourse with anyone other than Robert for the next fifteen years while they were married and living together, she would "sign all of her right, title and interest of any marital property" to Robert, and in exchange he would pay her $10,000 and an additional $1,000 annually for the next fifteen years. Barbara had another affair, Robert filed for the divorce, and the court upheld the post-nup as governed by contract law.

Though in these two cases the property clause only resulted in changes that were beneficial to the relationship in the short term, it can also motivate long-term behavioral change under the right circumstances. For the first few years of Dennis and Martha's marriage, things were great—Dennis was a young business executive who made a good living and Martha was a teacher who enjoyed her job. They bought a wonderful house in a great suburb in anticipation of starting a family, and over the next seven years had three children. Martha quit her job before the birth of their first child and was a stay-at-home mom. Though Dennis received two promotions and was earning a good salary, they had a sizeable mortgage payment and their real estate taxes had increased significantly, so money was tight. In part, this was the source of growing tension between Dennis and Martha. Increasingly, Dennis stayed late at the office and volunteered for assignments that required him to travel; he hated the arguments that had begun to define his relationship with his wife.

For her part, Martha was also struggling with the tension in their relationship and the negative effect it was having on their children. She vowed to do something about it, and what she did was create a post-nup with a lawyer's assistance. One part of the post-nup called for Dennis to lose all rights to the house in the event of a divorce and to move out immediately if divorce papers were filed. As much as Dennis hated agreeing to this part of the post-nup, Martha was insistent that this clause be included, and the last thing he wanted was to engage in another argument. As much as he hoped to save the marriage and return "to the way things used to be," Dennis was not particularly motivated to change—he liked his job and wondered if things might be better for both of them and the kids if they split up.

But over the next few months, during which he and Martha began marital counseling, Dennis began to think more seriously about what life would be like if a divorce were to occur. Every day when he left for the office and walked out of the house he loved, he thought to himself, *What if this were the last time that I woke up here?* It wasn't that he cared about the house more than Martha and the kids, but it was something tangible he could relate to losing. The more Dennis thought about being forced to move out, the more motivated he became to deal with the issues—financial and otherwise—that had hurt his relationship with Martha. It took almost a year, but the tension eventually dissipated to the point that the marriage was on solid ground and divorce was no longer a looming possibility.

When both people are trying to save the marriage, each has motivation to be fair. The post-nup may be created when one person is angry (at the other person's bad behavior) and the other feels guilty (for that behavior). Both of them, however, want to do whatever they can to save the marriage, and property becomes both carrot and stick motivation for couples—it's something that's meaningful to both of them and so carries motivational weight.

Reading this, you may be wondering why couples would wait until a difficult patch in their marriage to create a Property Pact. After all, given the relatively high rate of divorce, you would think such a pact might be standard operating procedure—or that couples would create a prenup precisely because they recognize that marriage is often a 50-50 proposition. At the start of a marriage, however, you may have relatively few material goods—you are renting instead of owning property, you possess modest savings, and your cars and other personal possessions aren't worth much. So at this point, it's difficult to create an agreement for something that you won't accumulate until what seems like far in the future.

From a psychological standpoint, couples are often reluctant to create prenup property divisions. When people are starting out as a couple, they are filled with optimism. The marriage is strong, and they can't conceive of a time when they're not happy and divorce becomes a possibility. In addition, creating a prenup where you start divvying up property seems like bad luck to many people. It's like you're putting a curse on the marriage before it even has a chance to get going. For these reasons, you're most likely to create a fair Property Pact mid-marriage rather than at its beginning or ending.

What Gets Divided

You can make the Property Pact as detailed as you'd like. For some couples, the key items are the residence and savings (investments as well as money in the bank), and these may be the only focus of the pact. Other couples may identify specific items of personal property, recognizing that these items can incentivize badly behaving spouses to change their ways.

For instance, Jim and Joan have been having marital problems, primarily because Jim is a physical fitness nut who spends the vast majority of his free time working out in the gym and participating in triathlons. His dedication to training for races has reached the point that Jim rarely is able to do much with his family on the weekends because of his exercise routine. Fed up with his behavior, Joan uses the post-nup to encourage Jim to change his routine. Using the Property Pact, she specifies that in the event of a divorce, specific assets will be sold and the income split 50/50. Among the assets is Jim's custom-made bike that cost $15,000. Knowing how much Jim values the bike, Joan specified it in the pact hoping that this divorce consequence will jar him into moderating his exercising and spending more time with the family.

Unlike Jim and Joan, some couples will agree to a split of property that favors one spouse over the other. Rather than the 50/50 division of marital property that is common in many states, couples may agree to pacts in which one spouse receives a greater share of assets than the other in response to the latter's counterproductive behaviors. If you are considering this type of pact, you and your spouse must consult attorneys to ensure that the pact stands a good chance of being approved by a judge. As I've noted earlier, judges will not honor post-nups that seem unconscionable or blatantly unfair to one party or that are in violation of state laws. Some state courts wouldn't enforce the Garner or Laudig agreements either because they would be viewed as unfair because they involved triggers based on conduct, or because the agreements could be viewed as penalties for seeking a divorce. Ideally, you should have an attorney create the Property Pact in a post-nup to avoid enforcement problems. If you write the pact yourself, you should have an attorney review it to make sure that the language doesn't create problems if you get divorced.

In certain ways, the Property Pact section of a post-nup is similar to wills or estate plans in that it can be amended based on changes that occur before the legal document goes into effect. In legal terms, this amended provision is a "supplement," and it allows couples to adjust the pact based on factors that affect what they own and their value as well as developments in the marriage. What is fair when one spouse is guilty of spending excessive amounts of money isn't fair when she has stopped this behavior. Let's say that the behavior imperiling the marriage is a spouse's spendthrift ways—she's maxed out the credit cards and incurred a lot of debt. As a result, the Property Pact states that she will receive less than her 50 percent share of the property if they divorce. In the next few years, though, this person changes her behaviors, learns to manage her spending, and the marriage is back on solid ground. Given that she has changed her behaviors to the satisfaction of her spouse and the betterment of the marriage, it's fair to amend the Property Pact to achieve a more equitable distribution of property. A post-nup can also contain contingencies triggering revision without amendment. For instance, one spouse can eliminate all her credit card debt by a targeted date, thereby making a given provision null and void.

Speaking of spending, the Property Pact can also address debts incurred during the marriage. Just as the law views anything purchased during the course of the marriage as marital property, it views any debts incurred as marital debt. A Property Pact, however, can divide responsibility for debt based on who incurred it. Similarly, it can give the financially responsible spouse veto power for all expenditures, mandating that this individual receive a copy of all credit card reports. It can also implement what I refer to as the Ralph Kramden Rule (Ralph was the bus driver husband on the old TV show *The Honeymooners*): the responsible spouse (i.e., wife Alice Kramden) gives the financially irresponsible spouse a spending allowance.

In fact, a pact may contain language to the effect that if one spouse files for personal bankruptcy, the other spouse is protected from the negative repercussions of this filing. While the financially responsible spouse can help pay down the debts her spouse has incurred, these payments become credits if a divorce ensues—meaning that the financially responsible spouse is compensated for all the debt she helped pay off.

The range of Property Pact options is necessarily wide, since couples have a variety of issues regarding money, residences, and the like. Tailoring a Property Pact to a specific situation enhances the pact's effectiveness, both as motivation against continued bad behavior and as a way to achieve a fair distribution of property if the relationship goes south. In one pact, a spouse may insist that his wife attend counseling to deal with her spending issues, and that if she doesn't, she will be responsible for all the excessive debt she has incurred. Another pact may focus on a spouse's refusal to obtain a job commensurate with his education, thus hurting the couple's ability to save and achieve other property-related goals.

For instance, Terry is a certified public accountant who decided to become a stay-at-home dad when he and his wife, June, had a child. Their child recently started school, but Terry is still primarily a homemaker who works just fifteen hours a week as a barista at a local coffee house. June, who makes a modest income as a paralegal, has urged Terry to obtain a full-time, better-paying job at an accounting firm, but he has refused because he likes staying home. As the couple's financial situation becomes more precarious, the tension between June and Terry increases, so she creates a Property Pact as part of a post-nup. In it, she lays out specific actions Terry must take within a one-year period to find an accounting position. The consequence of his not making a good faith effort to find that position will be a divorce in which he has to pay a significant amount of maintenance—and more to the point, one in which he will have to work full-time.

Identifying Income-Generating Responsibilities and Abilities

In the previous example, Terry wasn't accepting his financial responsibility to the marriage based on his ability. This is a common problem in marriages, and the Property Pact can help clarify this issue for both spouses, thus removing or diminishing a major source of stress in the marriage.

The pact can also help define responsibilities and abilities that affect maintenance payments after a divorce. Tammy is a doctor who worked in emergency rooms prior to her marriage to Bill, but she has only worked part-time since they had kids. This was fine with Bill, a successful businessman, and they have enjoyed a nice lifestyle despite Tammy's limited part-time income. As their relationship deteriorated, though, they created a post-nup, and the Property Pact included a clause that Tammy would waive her right to maintenance if they ended up getting divorced. They agreed to include this clause because both of them were aware that Tammy's experience as an ER doctor and the need for physicians with her expertise would enable her to obtain a good-paying, full-time job if she needed one.

On the other hand, consider Susan and Jeff: Susan hasn't worked in ten years and, unlike Tammy, has little experience or expertise that would help her land a decent-paying job. Thus, her pact with Jeff calls for her to receive maintenance of $2,000 monthly plus cost of living increases tied to the consumer price index so that she can return to school and finish her degree. Though Jeff earns $60,000 annually when the pact is written, there's no guarantee that he'll be making that amount at a point in the future when they might divorce, so the pact builds in a reduction if he's making less.

Property Pacts can be tweaked a number of different ways. An increasingly common situation involves a husband who is out of work and receiving unemployment while his wife works and supports the family. In a number of instances, the husband fails to pursue career opportunities vigorously (or doesn't pursue them at all), either because he refuses to settle for a "lesser" career path or because he's depressed from losing his job. Whatever the reason, the pact specifies that because he's failed to try to get a job, he will not receive maintenance and his share of the marital assets will be reduced by 15 percent.

Couples can also use the Property Pact to calculate cost-of-living expenses responsibly. For instance, let's say a husband smokes marijuana daily, and his habit costs the family $1,000 monthly. Though the wife's income pays for his marijuana, she is convinced smoking is a bad habit that's detrimental to their family. When they create their Property Pact, they agree to document this $1,000 monthly habit and note that this is not an "approved" living expense. Because of the pact, this amount won't be figured into their living expenses, ensuring that the wife will probably receive additional maintenance (because living expenses are a key calculation in maintenance determinations).

In the parlance of divorce, the expenditure on marijuana could be viewed as "dissipation"—the wasting of money. In this context, if the post-nup specified this habitual expenditure, a judge might consider the net asset picture differently. In divorce court proceedings, it's likely that the marijuana-using spouse will deny this behavior, so having it in the post-nup is essential.

Significant Assets

If you're poor or if you're young and have accumulated very little wealth (you're renting, your cars are old and worth little, you don't have much in terms of savings or investments), then this section isn't for you. On the other hand, even if you aren't a tycoon, the odds are that many of you have some property that's worth a decent amount of money, such as your home or retirement accounts. The more assets you possess, the more important the Property Pact is. Whatever your net worth may be, as long as you own a certain amount of "stuff"— residences, cars, consumer electronics—or have a decent amount of money saved or in benefit plans or investments, then you should be aware of how the Property Pact can work to your advantage.

- **Privacy.** By agreeing far in advance of a divorce to divvy up property in a specific way through the Property Pact, couples decrease the odds that what they own will become public knowledge. Admittedly, this is of much greater concern for the ultra-rich, since in nasty divorces, details of the demands and counter-demands of spouses are often leaked to the media. A Property Pact nails down how everything will be split far in advance of the divorce, making it far less likely that the divorce will become nasty and that the media will get wind that one spouse is demanding $1 million monthly in maintenance.

Privacy, though, is also a concern for people who aren't super rich. In contentious, vengeful divorces, people treat property like weapons: "You want a divorce, fine, then I'm going to tell everyone how you're screwing me and the kids over by forcing me to sell our house and split the money we get!" Typically, this speaker will tell the world—his family, her family, friends—of her spouse's treacherous act. The Property Pact resolves the division of assets before divorce-related anger can turn these assets into public weapons.

- **Fairness.** Some couples have accumulated some wealth and possessions during the course of their marriage, but the vast majority or all of it is due to one spouse's efforts. In fact, a primary motivation in creating the post-nup is the tension that results because one spouse not only refuses to get a job but also does little around the house and fails to take his child-raising responsibilities seriously. Jordan, for instance, was a fashion photographer who was passionate about his profession but made relatively little money from it. His wife, Denise, was a partner in a large law firm and worked tirelessly while also being the one who spent the most time taking their kids to soccer practice, making them dinner, and so on. While both Denise and Jordan want to make their marriage work, they realize that there is a decent chance that it won't, in large part because Jordan spends so much time away from home at fashion shows. When discussing the Property Pact, Jordan agreed to Denise's request that, in the event of a divorce, he will receive 40 percent of their assets and no maintenance. Jordan recognized that though the law might say that he should receive more, he acknowledged that the 40 percent figure was fair within the context of their relationship.

- **Estate planning.** For instance, you may own a second home and you and your spouse have always intended to pass it on to your children via an irrevocable trust and create a separate trust to fund maintenance and real estate taxes on this home. You may have other property, such as family heirlooms, that you and your spouse want to go to a given child. Whatever your intent is, you should codify it in the Property Pact. Divorce can wreak havoc with your mutual aim to pass on certain property to certain people. In addition to addressing these issues in the Property Pact, you may want to use estate planning to clarify your wishes. The two legal documents can complement each other to achieve goals when your relationship with your spouse is amicable (or at least better than it is during divorce proceedings). For example, the house you intend to pass down to the next generation should be excluded as an asset to be divided between you and your spouse. In terms of the estate, you can deed the second home to an irrevocable trust so that it is no longer controlled by either you or your spouse. That same transfer may place the second home outside of the estate for tax purposes.

- **Tax implications.** The Property Pact presents a great opportunity to deal with tax issues that may become thorny if the marriage can't be saved. For instance, if a couple gets divorced, should they file their last return jointly or separately? Or, in the event of a divorce, who will claim the dependency exemptions in a given year? Forging agreements on these tax issues during the post-nup phase removes a potentially stressful issue from the divorce discussions. Tax conflicts can be a source of tremendous animosity, and they can be used as bargaining chips by combative divorce attorneys. Therefore, if you can get them off the negotiating table in the Property Pact, you'll be much better off.

The Business Is Your Other Baby

In many contentious divorces, a particular object becomes a battleground. It may be a car, a house, or a work of art. This particular thing is no longer just an object but takes on symbolic weight—the emotional weight of the marriage. People argue about who gets the car, but it's not really the car that they're arguing about; the automobile serves as a forum to air grievances ("You don't care about the car; you just want it because you know how much I love it!") or express feelings ("You care more about the car than you do about me").

The Property Pact can help you remove this object from the divorce discussion. By mutually agreeing what will happen to that beautiful painting you bought on your honeymoon in France or the vacation house that has so many great memories or even the dog that you both love, you prevent a treasured object from turning into an object of enmity.

Perhaps the "object" that creates the most dissension in divorce discussions is a business. For one thing, it can be difficult to estimate the value of a business in order to divide the assets fairly. Ideally, a shareholder's agreement exists that contains a valuation method, and this method can be incorporated into the Property Pact. If not, the post-nup should include a provision that specifies how the company will be valued, facilitating the division of assets. In fact, valuation is a concept that couples should discuss even if neither one owns a business, since IRAs, Roths, and 401(k) plans also should be valued so their assets can be split equitably.

Arguments can rage in divorces not only about how much the business is worth but what is fair compensation for the non-business-owning spouse. If the agreement is that this non-owning spouse will not receive a share of the business after a divorce, then the issue is what constitutes fair compensation. Certainly valuing the business fairly and early in the process helps, but as you can imagine, the non-owning spouse may want more than fair value, especially if she blames the business for the divorce ("All you do is work!") or knows how much her spouse loves the business and wants to punish him for it. That's why the post-nup is the place to discuss what's fair compensation given all the issues involved: how much the non-owning spouse contributed to the business' success, how much she sacrificed in order to allow the business owner to make the company successful, and so on. Hammering out this agreement when there's still hope the marriage can be saved will result in terms that couples usually can both live with (and that a judge often finds acceptable) if a divorce results.

Pets Are Property

As you probably are aware, during a divorce people can fight over all sorts of possessions, from antiques to automobiles. People become emotionally attached to pieces of property and fight over them as if they're living things. One piece of property that can be the object of battles actually is a living thing: pets.

Americans love their pets and now have more pets per capita than at any time in history. Newly married couples often purchase pets together before they have children, and they are treated with great affection.

The law has started to recognize the importance of pets in our lives. Pets used to be valued simply as personal property under the law, no different than a hammer or a coat. Our firm received a significant amount of publicity when we recovered damages for a woman whose older dog was run over by a Waste Management truck while she was walking it. The damages reflected the court's view that the dog was worth far more than the typical piece of property; it was a valued member of the woman's family.

In an acrimonious divorce, pets can become pawns. If a husband knows that his wife loves the Persian cat, he may seek it in the divorce. If the wife knows that the husband thinks that Rover is the only being who understands him (and knows the burden of living with her), she may stake a claim to Rover.

The post-nup prevents couples from using pets as bargaining chips in a divorce, allowing them to designate who receives "custody" of the pet. It can also set terms for pet visitation. A couple can use a post-nup to address the breeding of a show pet or egg or sperm collection for future breeding. The couple can discuss breeding restrictions so as not to jeopardize the line. For example, they can provide each other with veto power over certain types of breeding.

To address the cost of caring for a pet, post-nups can make provision for "pet support." That is, one spouse will continue to contribute to the weekly costs of the pet for a certain period of time. If you own a pet who became ill and needed surgery or medication, you know how expensive pet ownership can be. A post-nup, therefore, can anticipate these health and support issues by determining who will pay what for care and feeding of the pet, as well as who will make decisions about expensive healthcare treatment and who should decide about end-of-life issues.

It's not over the top to suggest that a Property Pact clause involving pets may have a significant impact on behavioral change. In fact, some people would be more motivated to change marriage-destroying habits if they're denied favorable visitation for their pets than their children.

Assess Your Property Pact

How might a Property Pact help you avoid a nightmare divorce? Ideally, you'll never find out, in that the post-nup will prove useful in saving your marriage. If it doesn't, however, you can use the Property Pact in many different ways, depending on your particular situation. To help you assess that situation from a Property Pact standpoint, ask yourself the following questions.

- **What is the most meaningful possession(s) in your marriage for your spouse?** Is it the house, the car, money/investments, retirement accounts, and so on? Would the possibility of losing this prized possession motivate your spouse to change a behavior that is harming the marriage?
- **What do you own that you're most likely to argue about if you were to get divorced?** Can you make a list of all your major possessions and agree with your spouse on a 50/50 split for everything? Are there mitigating circumstances in which one of you should receive more than the other person? For instance, has either of you incurred individual debts that need to be addressed?
- **What is a fair split of your property, considering each of your financial responsibility versus your ability to fulfill that responsibility?** Have you or your spouse underperformed in terms of income based on your education and skills?

Has laziness, an inability to work well for or with others, or other factors caused one of you to contribute far less than you're capable of contributing? Once the safety net of one spouse making a good salary was removed, would the other spouse be able to secure a better-paying job than she had while you were married? Given all these issues, what is a fair split of property and what would be a fair amount of maintenance?

- **In the case of a significant amount of assets, does a Property Pact help you achieve the following goals if a divorce occurs?**
    1. Keeping the details of the divorce private (no family members, friends, or others knowing the details of what you own and how it's being divided)
    2. Making sure that your property is divided fairly according to you and your spouse, rather than as the law might dictate
    3. Addressing estate planning issues to ensure that the right property goes to the right kids at the right time
    4. Resolving tax questions regarding property that might become major issues if left until the time of divorce
- **Do you anticipate a particular object becoming a battleground if you were to divorce?** Is there an object that might take on powerful symbolic or emotional meaning and be something that generates furious arguments (such as a business owned by one of you)? What would be a fair way to value this object and make sure both of you receive appropriate compensation (e.g., one person receives ownership and the other receives roughly equal compensation)?

- **Do you have a pet to whom you're both emotionally attached?** Have you considered who would receive custody of the pet if you were to divorce and how visitation would work? Would including a behavior-related clause related to your pet motivate your spouse to change things he says or does that are harming the marriage?

7

The Custody Pact

Treat Kids with Care Before
They Become Weaponized

DIVORCE IS NOT KIND TO CHILDREN. You and your spouse may both be wonderful, loving parents, but the divorce process can turn even the best parents into people who inadvertently make decisions that are not in their kids' best interests. When you're enraged and vengeful, your primary goal may be to hurt your spouse in any way possible—including using the children as "weapons" to inflict emotional injury. This may also be your spouse's motivation during the divorce process. While such vindictiveness may not seem like a possibility at the moment, be aware that once you move into divorce territory, it's not an uncommon motivation.

In acrimonious divorces, rationality often goes out the window. When you discover that your spouse has been lying to you for the past ten years about your finances or you find out that he's had numerous affairs, you have every right to be angry and vengeful. Ideally, these feeling would be vented and dealt with in therapy. Too often, however, they become behavioral drivers as you battle over visitation, custody, and other matters. Some aggressive attorneys only exacerbate vengeful feelings, and their clients lose sight of what's important or rationalize their scorched-earth strategies.

If you can address custody-related issues while you're still on relatively good terms with your spouse, everyone benefits. Most obviously, you'll both consistently put you children's welfare first rather than take actions based on your or your spouse's desire for vengeance. Custody Pacts, though, also benefit you and your spouse, forging agreements that are fair and increasing the odds that you both can work together as part of a child's team after a divorce rather than fighting constantly and stressfully. You will also increase the chances that the Custody Pact that you create will be enforced by a judge. The judge's only consideration will be whether the arrangements reached are in the best interests of the children.

Even though custody and visitation are the most important decisions in any divorce, many people don't want to talk about Custody Pacts because they're operating under a misconception.

Everyone Knows My Spouse Shouldn't Get the Kids

The misconception that many people act under is that the law is all-seeing and all-knowing. A person whose spouse has been using drugs or drinking to excess or has gambled away the family's entire life savings assumes that the court will recognize a spouse's bad behavior and punish him for it: the courts couldn't possibly let such an irresponsible and reckless person see the kids unsupervised.

Unfortunately, what you know to be true and what you can prove legally are often two different things. We tend to forget that our family life is far more private than we assume. If you've ever had friends who have gotten divorced, you probably were surprised at least half the time; you figured that they had a decent marriage. Then, when your friend confides in you after the divorce that her spouse was a gambling addict and buried the family in debt, you're shocked. Similarly, the outside world probably knows little about your spouse's misbehaviors. Unless you've made it a point to gather evidence systematically—recording incriminating episodes of pulling into the driveway drunk, saving e-mails in which he admits to drug use—you may find yourself struggling to make your case to a judge.

It is important note here that if the behavior in question is physical abuse of either you or your children, your first priority should be the physical safety and well-being of all of you. Once you are removed from any physical threats, you can consult with appropriate professionals to see if the marriage should be saved or how best to address custody matters.

Judges are well aware that some people make false claims of bad behavior as a legal tactic. Just because you say it's so and because "everyone knows" that your spouse is a drunk doesn't mean that you can convince a judge of this misbehavior or that your spouse will be denied custody because of it.

Judges also know that during divorce cases, some angry spouses may demand sole custody even when they don't want it or insist on supervised visitation to humiliate their soon-to-be ex. For instance, a parent may request a rigid visitation schedule knowing that this will inconvenience the other parent who has moved thirty miles away or make it impossible for him to see his child regularly.

If you put yourself in the place of family law judges, you can understand how difficult it is for them to make a fair decision based on your charges without solid evidence. These judges have seen everything, and they know that divorcing couples will lie and deceive because they're in the grip of divorce court insanity. They are all too well aware that some people act in ways that they ordinarily wouldn't because the process makes them temporarily crazy.

For this reason, judges may grant joint custody to a spouse who has a problem with alcohol or who is not sufficiently responsible or present to have equal parenting status. With a Custody Pact in place, on the other hand, judges often possess the evidence they need to make a decision that is in the best interest of the children.

Why Misbehaving Spouses Agree to Custody Pacts

Admittedly, couples may find it difficult to hammer out agreements regarding custody arrangements when they're trying to save the marriage. It's an awkward conversation to have because these are emotion-laden issues, and it may be painful to talk about a future in which the kids are living with one spouse and not the other.

But many couples will realize it's a conversation that's better to have sooner rather than later. In fact, for couples going through an acrimonious divorce, it's unrealistic to expect them to put all their resentment, anger, and disappointment aside and discuss custody rationally. When people think about it—or talk about it with divorced friends who have fought over custody and visitation—they usually grasp that it's better to create agreement on these issues while the marriage is still viable.

Custody Pact discussions should remain focused on what is best for the children and what is realistic, given future circumstances. If, for instance, Dad has always been a secondary caregiver because he travels a lot for work and will continue to do so in the future, joint custody or shuffling kids back and forth between each parent's residence probably doesn't make sense. Similarly, if the marriage is rocky because of a parent's alcohol or drug addiction, then the non-offending parent should receive custody and even visitation should be limited or supervised. Conversely, if both parents have shared responsibility for raising the children and the type of misbehavior the post-nup is attempting to rectify is not one that has a negative effect on the children, then joint custody is an option. In addition, issues such as whether the children should split time in each parent's residence and who will supervise the kids in each residence when Mom or Dad isn't there (grandparents, babysitters, etc.) can be addressed.

Let me repeat my earlier warning: it's very difficult to talk about these issues with the children's best interests in mind during a heated divorce. No doubt, people convince themselves that they are putting the children first when they argue for a custody arrangement during the divorce, but too often they are arguing from a hostile and often illogical position. Some couples can project into the future and realize that if the worst happens, they will not be in an emotional state that guarantees the best interests of their children will be served. The following hypothetical case history illustrates this point.

Sue and Andrew were having a tough time in their marriage because Andrew had an affair. Even though Andrew claimed the affair was over, Sue wasn't so sure if her husband was telling the truth—this was the second affair that he had had during their ten-year marriage. Still, he begged her to give him a third chance, and Sue said that the only way she would do so is if he agreed to a post-nup. Sue had leverage at this point in time, and Andrew was motivated to make concessions in order to preserve the marriage. As part of the post-nup, they created a Custody Pact in which Andrew admitted that he had been a negligent parent—besides his affairs, he rarely attended his children's parent-teacher conferences or their events at school—and he agreed not to seek joint custody if he and Sue were to divorce.

Andrew agreed to this Custody Pact in part because he wanted to make the marriage work, but also because he felt guilty about his behaviors and the effects they had on his kids. Other mothers and fathers are also not in denial about their issues. Some people are able to recognize that it would be a mistake for them to have custody if they continue drinking to excess or abusing drugs. Even if they're not guilty of these egregiously offensive behaviors, they may acknowledge that they are not as responsible of a parent as their spouse and therefore be willing to agree to a pact that will be best for their kids.

Keep in mind that Custody Pacts also offer misbehaving spouses a chance to prove that they're serious about changing and preserving the marriage. They can prove their sincerity by agreeing to give up joint custody or to restrictions on their visitation if they don't change. They recognize that the pact represents a last window of opportunity, and it's no longer enough that they make another empty promise about making more time to be with the family or stopping gambling. They know they need strong motivation to make the behavioral adjustments their spouse requires (and that they probably accept are fair), and the Custody Pact provides this motivation.

Additional Advantages

Beyond helping parents create fair custody arrangements that are in the best interests of their children, Custody Pacts allow parents to deal with a variety of divorce-related situations that can become nightmarish. Let's look at two key benefits.

• **Managing post-divorce logistical issues.** Anticipating and addressing the logistical issues of joint custody in a post-nup can minimize the stress during a divorce as well as the fights and bitterness that may occur afterward. For instance, in today's environment, many working parents aren't tied to nine-to-five schedules. Some work seven days a week, ten hours a day; others travel constantly; still others are independent contractors and often don't know from week to week what their work schedule will be. All this makes it easy for a vindictive spouse to take revenge by insisting on a visitation schedule that she knows her ex won't be able to adhere to because he sometimes has to work weekends. Thus, he may have to miss as many as half of his scheduled weekends with his kids.

Using a Custody Pact, this couple can address the constraints on each of their schedules and agree to a custody and visitation arrangement that takes these schedules into consideration. Ideally, they will build in flexibility to this arrangement, creating a provision that if a spouse has to work on a given day, he will be given a makeup day later on.

Similarly, let's say that a spouse knows that he's going to be asked to relocate out of state for his job. Given most state laws, this relocated spouse will see his children far less frequently than he should; he essentially will be "punished" for moving to a different location. Even though our society has become more geographically diverse, courts often deny a spouse custody if she moves for a job. Or, if the child were to move with the mother, the child would not be readily accessible to the father. In the Custody Pact stage, couples often can talk about this issue rationally, accepting that it would not be good for the children to be denied access to either parent for an extended period of time. The pact can take the possibility of relocation into consideration, stating that if it occurs, the kids will spend part of the summer with the geographically distant parent or that a budget will be set up to pay for weekend trips, either the parent visiting the children in the custodial parent's residence or the children visiting the relocated parent.

- **Figuring out future financial decisions affecting the children.** Who is going to pay for college? Should a child be allowed to go to any university or will only schools within a certain price range be considered? What about graduate school? Given the already steep costs of college and the likelihood that they will continue to increase, the questions posed here need to be answered before a divorce occurs. This will allow parents to arrive at the right answers together, since they know a lot more about their situations—their present and potential future income, their kids and what schools might serve them best—than the courts do. During an acrimonious divorce, these future financial questions often become strategic weapons for each side to use as bargaining chips. As a result, decisions are made legally rather than with the specifics of parental income and children's interests and situations in mind.

Set the Record Straight

A Custody Pact may not save your marriage, but it provides both you and your spouse with a chance to be honest with each other—and ultimately with the court—about your abilities as parents. This honesty is crucial for your children and hard to achieve if divorce proceedings are initiated.

Without this honesty, you are vulnerable to using all sorts of tactics that are designed to satisfy a need for vengeance or to be used as leverage in order to gain a more favorable settlement. Even if these tactics are effective in the short run, they create long-term animosity between you and your ex that will result in ongoing battles and stress for years. More important, these tactics often deprive children of time with you or your spouse—time that is critical to their growth and development.

As we noted earlier, false charges aren't uncommon as a legal tactic. Even more commonly, your spouse may take a single, isolated incident from your past and use it to demonstrate why you shouldn't have joint custody or why your visitation should be limited and supervised. For instance, two years ago you were on the road frequently because of your job, and there was one stretch when you were out of the country for an entire month. During the divorce proceedings, your angry spouse claims that you were an "absentee" father who shirked his responsibility as a parent. Even if this charge is completely false, a judge may give it credibility because of that one period of time when you were physically absent.

A Custody Pact can take the possibility of vindictive, counterproductive charges like these off the table. Of course, if you're married to someone who is in fact absent, addicted to drugs or alcohol, or a bad parent in any other way, you don't want to make a false statement in a Custody Pact about his fitness as a parent. If both you and your spouse are good parents, however, you should include the following in a Custody Pact:

- Mutual statements attesting to your fitness as parents
- Declarations that neither of you are abusive, are addicted to drugs or alcohol, or have harmed your children in any way
- Acknowledgement that though one or both of you have been absent occasionally from the home because of work demands, you both are present and involved in your children's lives as much as possible

Assess Your Custody Pact

The following assesment questions are designed to help you determine how a Custody Pact might benefit you, your marriage, and your children if a divorce takes place.

- **Do you assume you will be granted custody?** Do you believe that there's no way that your spouse will be granted sole or joint custody because "everyone knows" he's not an involved or responsible parent? Do you make this assumption even though there isn't evidence you can present in court to this effect?

- **Would your spouse be willing to agree to custody restrictions within a post-nup?** For example, would he agree to a Custody Pact that places restrictions on visitation or prevents him from having joint custody in the event of a divorce because of his bad behaviors? Would he accept these provisions in exchange for you giving him a second chance to change and make the marriage work? Might he agree to them because he loves his kids and wants to do what's best for them?

- **If you were to divorce, might logistical difficulties arise?** Consider this in terms of when you or your spouse could be with your children (e.g., picking them up from school, taking care of them on weekends). Do you anticipate that you and your ex may disagree about who should pay for schooling (private or religious schools, college, grad school)? Are you concerned about protecting your kids from your spouse's harmful behaviors?

- **Do you believe your spouse is a fit parent?** If you were to create a Custody Pact today, while the possibility of saving the marriage still exists, would your spouse be willing to attest to your fitness as a parent? Would you be willing to attest to his fitness?

8

Tactical Applications

Solving the Nine Common Marital
Problems—Plus One

A CCORDING TO THE AMERICAN ACADEMY OF MATRIMONIAL
LAWYERS (AAML), marriages fail for nine common reasons.
While post-nups can't always prevent these failures, they can help
couples raise awareness of key issues, explore options to deal with
them, and take actions that may defuse tensions or stop problems
from reaching the critical stage.

Each of the components of a post-nup—the Action Pact, Property
Pact, and Custody Pact—can be employed to solve marital problems.
In earlier chapters, we touched on how they can be used to confront a
variety of issues that can hurt the marriage, from addictions to infidelity
to absence. Though I've discussed some of these issues previously, I'm
going to focus on them in a much more prescriptive way here—suggesting how tactical applications of post-nups can help resolve the
problems or moderate the damage they do to a marriage. Let's look at
the nine failure factors identified by the AAML as well as a "plus one"
category I've added to cover three additional causes of failed marriages:

1. Poor communication
2. Financial problems
3. A lack of commitment to the marriage
4. A dramatic change in priorities
5. Infidelity
6. Failed expectations or unmet needs
7. Addictions and substance abuse
8. Physical, sexual, or emotional abuse
9. Lack of conflict resolution skills
10. Plus one

Poor Communication

As I've noted earlier, many marriages flounder due to a lack of communication or because of miscommunication. While it's possible that two people just aren't on the same wavelength and never will be, many times the cause of poor communication is based on personality differences or related to changes in circumstance. In terms of the former, introverts often are reluctant or unable to express their true feelings to spouses (or to other people, for that matter). Others persist in maintaining their desired persona even when doing so strains credulity. In a personal injury case our firm handled, a man lost a finger in a workplace accident. We asked him how he felt about it, and he replied, establishing his tough-guy credentials, "I can get by; I have nine other fingers."

As you might imagine, this macho attitude may be admirable in one sense (guys who don't whine about their misfortunes) but may also destroy a marriage. Vince, for instance, was fired from his job at a Fortune 500 corporation but never complained about it to his wife, Ginny. On many occasions, Ginny tried to get him to open up about how disappointed he was in being let go and how anxious he was as his unemployment stretched from weeks to months, but

Vince maintained his strong, silent posture. However, he also became distant and uncommunicative not only with Ginny but with their three children. He refused to go to marriage counseling or see an individual therapist, and eventually Ginny filed for divorce because, as she noted, "the man I married has become a robot."

Changing circumstances, too, can affect communication for both men and women. For example, a couple has children, and they decide that Mom should quit her job and stay home with the kids while Dad continues to work. Dad feels increased pressure to do well at work and receive salary increases and bonuses, while Mom feels isolated from the adult world. Both of them, however, don't communicate their fears and concerns because they don't want to whine about the roles they've accepted. Unfortunately, their inability to communicate what's going on in their heads and their dissatisfaction with their roles can eat away at the marriage and prevent them from exploring other more relationship-healthy solutions.

The ability to adapt as situations change is the hallmark of good marriages, and strong communication facilitates this adaptive process. Creating a post-nup encourages a couple to express their feelings, both verbally and in writing. It may allow one or both spouses to level with their partners about their behaviors and what's upsetting them, it may lead to a discussion of alternatives that can help solve marital problems, and it may cause couples to enter therapy or seek other forms of counseling that usually result in better communication. Ultimately, the post-nup requires a couple to agree to terms, and arriving at this agreement means that spouses must learn to listen well and express themselves honestly and clearly.

If you doubt that communication is important to dealing with marital problems, consider a study conducted by University of North Carolina clinical psychology professor Donald Baucom in which couples experiencing marital discord were trained in communication skills. As part of the training, couples were taught to state a problem in clearly agreed-upon terms and then discuss the problem and options for behavioral change until a solution was reached. Other couples were taught another problem-solving/communication skill. And a third control group was set up that received no training.

The group that received the most communication skill training saw the greatest improvement in their marriages, while the control group saw no improvement.

Here are some examples of communication-related clauses that might be included in an Action Pact:

• Spouses agree to spend one hour every week to air their concerns, disappointments, and desires and to discuss their feelings honestly.

• Spouses make a commitment to attend therapy together that will facilitate open and continuous exchanges about specific issues in their marriage.

Financial Problems

As I've noted earlier, money disagreements and difficulties can create tremendous stress in a marriage. From conflict over credit card debt to anger about failures to save money, these issues can be far more detrimental to a marriage than they might appear. As much as we like to think that a strong marriage can survive problems as seemingly superficial as those involving money, many marriages crumble because of years of financially erosive behaviors.

Being aware of the range of problems—and shaping a post-nup to address them—is crucial. I've emphasized many of these problems in previous examples, but here is a quick summary of five of the most common financial issues that damage a marriage.

• **Reaganesque battles.** As you may recall, former President Reagan hit upon a strategy of spending a significant amount of the budget on the military so that there would be relatively few resources remaining for various social programs. In the same way, some spouses spend family money on certain items or in certain narrow areas (entertainment, the children, etc.) knowing that these expenditures will leave little cash available for other purchases. In other words, the spouse spends the money first and fast, creating tremendous tension with the non-spending partner.

- **Inequities.** These could result from a working spouse who makes all the major financial decisions because he's working and his wife is not; she feels she almost has to beg him for money and that he's a control freak when it comes to financial choices. It may also be that one spouse has a lot of money through an inheritance and dictates financial terms to her spouse because she is the one who brought all the money to the marriage. These inequities create tension between spouses because it seems unfair that one person dominates financial decision-making.

- **Hidden assets.** Sometimes motives are nefarious—people who stash money in accounts that are unknown to spouses because they use it for illicit purposes (gambling, drugs, etc.) or because they are planning for a divorce. In some instances, however, the motivation may be to save up for a big purchase and provide a happy surprise. It may be that someone feels he is smarter about money matters than his spouse and thinks that their finances are best served if he manages them on his own. Any of these situations is rife for conflict when the assets become known to the previously in-the-dark spouse.

- **Earning choices.** The arguments here might involve who works and who stays home with the children; or whether both spouses need to work when one would prefer to stay home. There can also be conflict if one person has made a job or career decision that limits her income, perhaps in favor of greater work satisfaction or flexibility. In any of these instances, the amount of income generated by couples can create escalating tension in a marriage, especially when additional income is needed, such as for funding children's education, paying medical bills, and so on.

- **Saving and spending clashes.** This is probably the most common area of disagreement, and it can include everything from a husband maxing out the credit cards to a wife who exhibits miserly behaviors. Over time, these conflicts can escalate in intensity. What once was merely irritating and the cause of bickering becomes highly stressful and the source of intense verbal battles.

At the very least, a post-nup can help couples deal with these five common issues by creating a financial plan that can be incorporated into the Action Pact—such a plan would address saving rates, spending limits, budgets, financial goals, and so on. Such a plan may also stipulate that a third-party advisor be hired to help the couple negotiate solutions to their conflicts—the post-nup may state that the couples will abide by the budget that this advisor helps them craft.

In addition, by coordinating the Action Pact and Property Pact sections of a post-nup, couples can ensure a fair outcome if a divorce occurs. Typically, a spouse who wastes a couple's assets through his excessive spending still receives half of everything upon divorce. Similarly, if this individual creates significant debt, the amount owed is split evenly when the relationship ends. A post-nup can help create a more equitable division of assets in these cases. As part of the post-nup, couples can agree that if specific marriage-damaging behaviors don't cease (e.g., excessive spending) and a divorce ensues, then the offending spouse will receive a smaller percentage of assets than the norm.

Nicole Needham Faidi and William Faidi created a post-nup in 2004 at Nicole's instigation; she was concerned that her husband, a real estate developer, was incurring debt that she would end up being responsible for. William had borrowed over $2 million from his parents and had negative net worth of $843,000 when he and Nicole created their post-nup. The post-nup stated that the couple would have no common property and Nicole wouldn't be responsible for any of William's financial obligations; it also stipulated that if the courts were to find that Nicole did have an obligation, that William would pay it. For seven years, this agreement helped hold the marriage together, but in 2011, Nicole filed for divorce, and the post-nup protected her from liability related to William's debts.

Debt protection is just one of many clauses that might be written into an Action Pact. Here are some others:

- Spouse A will spend no more than 5 percent of the couple's yearly gross salary on clothing.
- Spouse A will limit credit card charges to a maximum of $1,000 monthly.
- Spouse A agrees that Spouse B should work a part-time job, as long as Spouse B agrees to work less than twenty hours weekly.
- Spouse A will put 10 percent of the couple's yearly gross salary into a joint savings account, stock account, or certificate of deposit.

A Lack of Commitment to the Marriage

Sometimes, lack of commitment means the marriage is over except for the shouting—and the filing of papers. In many cases, however, a lack of commitment can represent a fixable problem. It may be that one or both spouses are just going through the motions because of what psychologists call habituation—they've been together long enough that they're taking each other for granted. Hal, for instance, had been married to Jasmine for seven years, and they had a three-year-old child. Hal complained to his friends that he still loved Jasmine but that "the spark was gone from their relationship." He began spending more time at work, at his health club, and with his friends, showing up for dinner a few nights a week and watching sports at home on Sundays. But he no longer scheduled date nights with Jasmine or proactively suggested they do much together as a family. Jasmine accused Hal of "going through the motions of a marriage," and though he protested, he knew that he wasn't as involved and actively committed to the relationship as he had been as little as two years ago. It was only when Jasmine presented Hal with a post-nup and she insisted that he make specific behavioral changes—one date night per week, three out of five weeknight dinners at home, one weekend family activity—that the harsh reality of the situation hit him. As Jasmine told him, if he was not willing to demonstrate his commitment to the marriage, then she would file for a divorce. If, on the other hand, he wanted to try to make the marriage work, he would commit to doing what she requested. If he failed in this commitment, he would have to pay an additional amount of maintenance when they divorced.

While it's impossible to "enforce" commitment in a loveless marriage, it is possible to send a powerful reminder that this commitment is necessary when love still exists. If a couple still cares deeply for each other, a post-nup can help get them back on the right path. The key, though, is that the post-nup must demand that the uncommitted spouse demonstrate a renewed commitment through specific actions. If the post-nup merely requires verbal reassurances, then it's unlikely that it will be effective. It's the combination of an Action Pact's insistence on new behaviors and a Property Pact's statement of financial consequences if these behaviors aren't undertaken that can generate commitment.

Here are some examples of commitment-catalyzing behaviors that an Action Pact can include:

- Being home for dinner at least twice a week
- Attending no fewer than half of all their son's basketball games

- Taking no fewer than two family vacations of at least five days each annually
  - Helping the kids with their homework at least once per week
  - Arranging date nights three times per month

A Dramatic Change in Priorities

In most instances, a marriage begins with the couple sharing life priorities. They both agree that they want to establish themselves in their careers; next, they want to buy a house; third, they want to start a family. Both proceed on the same track until things change. It may be an internal change like a midlife crisis or an external one like a sick parent in need of care. Whatever the cause, one spouse puts X first, while the other spouse prioritizes Y. This creates conflict and, if unaddressed, can lead to divorce.

Jody was married to Fred for twenty-five years, and though their marriage had its ups and downs, they raised two children successfully and it seemed like they were in it for the long haul. Fred was a corporate executive who made a good living, and Jody stayed home to take care of the children. When their kids left for college, though, Jody entered medical school and shortly after graduating landed a good job with a top hospital. For the first time in her life, Jody was making a good salary and pursuing a professional career. Fred, on the other hand, was contemplating early retirement and talking about how much he wanted to travel. Both their priorities had shifted, and initially, it was Jody who suggested they get a divorce despite the fact that they still loved each other. She said that their lives had moved in such different directions that she didn't see how they could stay married. After seeing how adamant Jody was about getting a divorce, Fred agreed that it was the right thing to do.

But was it? Fred and Jody could have put together a post-nup with the following terms:

• Fred can retire or work a few days a week, as he prefers.

• Jody gets to pursue her dream job, but agrees to accompany Fred on the exotic trips that Fred longs to take to New York, Paris, Rio, and London.

• Jody understands that Fred may take trips without her.

• Fred understands that Jody will work long hours during the week and often won't be back in time for usual dinners; she will only cook the great meals that he loves during the work week.

• Fred agrees that it is his turn to support Jody's career, and he will attend dinners with colleagues and association events to help Jody progress as a doctor.

Major life events often cause a spouse's priorities to shift. Early in a marriage, this event may be having children, new job demands, or increasing financial pressures. Later in a marriage, the events may involve illness or death of loved ones, the need to relocate for career purposes, or even retirement. Whatever the cause is, couples can discuss and negotiate shifting priorities through a post-nup. These discussions alert a spouse that his priorities have shifted and communicate that this shift had affected his spouse adversely. They also focus attention on the need for new behaviors so that this spouse can get his priorities aligned with his partner so that the marriage can continue.

Here are three examples of the types of priority-related issues that can be addressed in an Action Pact:

• Supporting (emotionally, financially, and in other ways) a spouse who wants to return to school to obtain an undergraduate or advanced degree (since career has become a higher priority for her).

• Accepting a spouse's desire to ride a motorcycle and agreeing on an acceptable price for the bike to be purchased (in response to his midlife crisis priority shift in which he wants to live life to the fullest).

- Agreeing that a couple who have recently retired will play golf three times a week and spend two days fishing so they can prioritize each of their passions while spending time together.

Infidelity

According to some statistical estimates, 40 percent of women and 44 percent of men have affairs during their marriages. As we've discussed in previous chapters, these affairs cause or at least contribute to the end of relationships. In a significant percentage of these marriages, however, the affair doesn't have to be "fatal." Within the course of a relationship over an extended period of time, people make all sorts of big mistakes, including having an affair. In some instances, they are anomalies and don't represent the true nature of the relationship. If one of the spouses was willing and able to give the other spouse a second chance, the damage done might be repaired and the couple would enjoy a long and happy marriage.

Post-nups offer couples a second chance. Sometimes, this second chance is one that the cheating spouse capitalizes on to change his behaviors. Admittedly, however, it's difficult to give someone a second chance when he's committed such a disloyal, hurtful act. A post-nup, however, places conditions on that second chance—conditions that involve consequences for not adopting new behaviors or for repeating the same unethical behavior. This usually creates far better outcomes than therapy, where people talk out their feelings and some cheating spouses promise never to cheat again, only to think, *I got away with it this time; why can't I get away with it again?*

Post-nups send a clear message that behaviors must change, cheating will not be tolerated, and that there are serious financial and other consequences if a spouse violates the post-nup agreement and they divorce.

Here are some examples of the type of clauses related to infidelity that can be included in an Action Pact:

- The cheating spouse agrees never to cheat again.
- The cheating spouse agrees never to communicate via text, e-mail, phone, or in person with the person he had an affair with.
- The non-cheating spouse is allowed to review her husband's texts and e-mails regularly for the first year this document is in effect.
- The cheating spouse will attend marriage counseling with his partner for one year.
- The cheating spouse must attend a sex addiction clinic to help deal with the issues that cause him to have affairs.

Failed Expectations or Unmet Needs

When people get married, they often share hopes and dreams. They both have their hearts set on owning a beautiful condo in the city and a second home in the country; they both want to have three kids and take European vacations. They also may have expectations of themselves (I expect to be CEO of my company by age fifty) and each other (I expect that we'll raise our children in the town where I grew up). Over time, though, some of these expectations don't become realities and needs go unmet. As a result, the marriage becomes stressed to the point that one or both spouses are unhappy and considering divorce.

For instance, Jill married Roger, a business consultant. They agreed that when they had children, Jill would stop working as a dentist and stay home to raise the children, which is exactly what happened. Things went well for a while, but then Roger began consulting in a sector that required him to attend numerous social events—and the expectation was that his wife would attend a number of these events with him. Jill quickly tired of the social whirl and being seen as "secondary" to Roger, and she refused to go to any more events. Roger was upset at her refusal, not only because her attendance was expected by existing and potential clients but because other consultants' spouses routinely joined their mates at events. Why was Jill being so difficult?

The problem was that neither Roger nor Jill had communicated their expectations to each other throughout their marriage. Roger wasn't aware that Jill was feeling unfulfilled and unchallenged and that being a social companion only made her feel worse; Jill was unaware that Roger was under tremendous pressure to bring in new clients and that these social functions were essential to achieve that goal.

As our earlier section noted, post-nups open the lines of communication in a marriage and keep them open. When Roger can say to Jill, "I really need you to attend at least half of these functions with me or my career at the firm will be in trouble," she will grasp what he needs from her and why. When Jill can articulate her feelings of isolation and lack of fulfillment, Roger can see how his wife wants more from life than she's getting and that these social events make her unmet expectations even more painful. It may be that they can't find a compromise so they both get all of their needs met, but the post-nup provides a forum for exploring alternatives and compromises—maybe Jill will agree to go to 50 percent of the functions and Roger will agree to stay home with the kids on weekends so Jill has time to work on a start-up business related to her dentistry credentials.

Here are some examples of the types of clauses related to failed expectations or unmet needs that might be included in an Action Pact:

- A working spouse agrees to provide his non-working spouse with financial, emotional, and childcare support so she can return to school and start to realize her unmet career goals.

- One spouse agrees to spend at least thirty minutes weekly discussing problems with their kids so that the entire responsibility of making some tough decisions doesn't fall on the other spouse.

- The spouses agree that they will actively plan one fun activity for themselves as a couple and one for themselves and their kids weekly in order to put more "fun and play" back in their lives.

Addictions and Substance Abuse

Sometimes, people are behaving so badly that a divorce rather than a post-nup is the right response. Some people just can't be helped, and if you're married to a hardcore addict, it may mean the end of your marriage. Fortunately, healthcare professionals have made strides in treating a variety of addictions, and it may be that your spouse can benefit from them if he admits he has a problem and is willing to explore treatment options with you as well as what needs to be done outside of therapeutic settings to manage his addiction.

Perhaps the most valuable aspect of a post-nup when it comes to addictions is that it links money and behaviors. For instance, spouses may write a post-nup that includes a clause that estimates the amount of money that one spouse has spent on drugs or alcohol, and then states that if a divorce takes place, she will give up that amount in assets to "even the balance." When people realize the true cost of their addictions and that there is a real price to pay if they can't get them under control, they are motivated to change their behaviors. While some courts may not enforce this type of clause, enlightened courts will.

In a way, post-nups are a form of intervention; they let the addict know that his behavior is hurting others and his marriage, and that he must seek help until the addictive behavior is under control. As in any intervention, consequences exist if the addict fails to adhere to the plan set forth in the post-nup—consequences that include divorce and other negative repercussions (e.g., agreed-upon language in the post-nup regarding past addictive conduct that could cause a judge to impose loss of custody).

Here are some examples of addiction-related clauses that can be included in the Action Pact:

- Spouse A agrees to enroll in an inpatient alcoholic rehabilitation facility for no fewer than thirty days.

- Spouse A agrees to attend AA meetings no fewer than three times weekly.

- Spouse A agrees that if a relapse occurs and the cocaine use continues, Spouse B will take control of all the couple's financial accounts.

Physical, Sexual, or Emotional Abuse

Your first priority must be to make sure you and your children are safe from physical or mental harm. Once you are safe, please work with appropriate professionals to see if a post-nup is right for your situation.

Lack of Conflict Resolution

In business, partners need to resolve differences in order to keep the business going. Say one partner wants to reduce his hours by 50 percent, yet he feels he is still entitled to half the profits. In this instance, partners must consider various alternatives and find a compromise—for example, the partner who works less agrees to reduce his profit percentage by 8 percent. They're able to arrive at a compromise and resolve their conflict because they're motivated to do so—they want to keep the business going because it's profitable and they enjoy running it. Contractually, they have to resolve conflicts, and if they can't, they must sell the business or shut it down.

Examples of marital conflicts abound. Tim is Jewish and Barb is Catholic. When they have kids, they find themselves arguing about the faith in which they'll raise the children, and over time, the conflict becomes the source of tremendous hostility on both their parts. Or Mark and Fran have a conflict about where they'll live—they both had jobs in Milwaukee, but Fran has received a terrific job offer from a company in Chicago and wants them to relocate there. They talk about the issue but each one just digs in deeper; they each become adamant that their position is the right one and are increasingly strident in their arguments.

While conflicts are an inevitable part of marriage and can be as major as religious divides and as minor as who takes out the trash, they need to be addressed and resolved rather than allowed to fester and infect the marriage. Post-nups provide a forum for addressing and resolving conflicts. By their very nature, they require couples to explore alternatives and compromises, and then formalize them within a legal document so that there are consequences for not sticking with the compromises agreed upon.

By being creative in post-nup discussions, couples can arrive at solutions that may not have occurred to either of them when they were arguing emotionally about an issue. While some couples will use a post-nup to bring a mediator or therapist into the process to help them work out a conflict, others can explore innovative alternatives. For example, I have married friends who are Muslim and Catholic, and they resolved their religious conflicts by agreeing to celebrate all their holidays and teaching their kids about both religions. I know of a similar marriage in which the couple resolved their conflicts by agreeing not to observe any religious holidays and to raise their children without any religion. Similarly, couples who work in different cities learn to make a go of their geographical dislocation through innovative commuter marriages—they agree to live in each other's cities on alternative weekends and use Skype and other virtual tools to talk regularly. Some simply agree to live at a midpoint between both jobs so that they are equally inconvenienced.

Here are some examples of conflict resolution clauses that can be included in an Action Pact:

- Both spouses agree to use an outside professional—therapist, coach, or mediator—when conflicts arise over given subjects.

- Spouse A and Spouse B agree to come up with a list of five alternatives whenever disagreements about their children's religious training arises.

Plus One: Battles About Sexual Preferences, Politics, and Child Raising

I've added three areas to the AAML's factors but I could easily have added ten. Marriages can be threatened for an astonishingly wide range of reasons, from a spouse's development of agoraphobia to a couple's decision to move to an exotic destination far from friends and family. But I've found that the following three factors can be especially problematic for couples today, so let's look at each and how a post-nup might be used to resolve the problems they raise.

- **Sexual preferences.** He wants to have sex every night, she thinks twice a week is pushing it. He wants to keep the relationship monogamous while she wants it to be open. He prefers the missionary position while she likes to be on top. He says she's frigid while she claims he's a sex addict.

I don't think I need to elaborate on all the other potential areas of sexual conflict except to note that as exotic as they might be, the problem usually comes down to meeting the needs of your partner. To resolve these conflicts, conversation and compromise are often necessary. While therapy can achieve these goals, couples are often reluctant to discuss these problems with any outsider, even a professional.

A post-nup serves as a conversation-starter, demonstrating how serious a sexual problem is—an important point, since one person may not be heeding his partner's complaints because he thinks "she'll get over it" and "it's not that big of a deal." When the prospect of divorce is raised, however, no one can mistake the problem as being minor or passing. A post-nup allows couples to forge agreements about the conflict. For instance, for couples who have different frequency preferences, the post-nup presents a compromise—four times a week rather than two or seven.

Someone once asked me if a post-nup might include a trigger clause related to sex. For instance: "If John doesn't change his behavior and have sex with me every night, he will forfeit his financial interest in the proceeds from the sale of our house in the event of a divorce." My experience is that judges would laugh this clause out of court. Judges tend to believe that what occurs in the bedroom between spouses has no place in court.

- **Politics.** Arguments ensue about all sorts of political races. Admittedly, politics stir passions, and they can create deep divides, especially when a former Republican becomes a Democrat (or vice versa). An individual may question if this is the person she married, if her spouse has lost his mind and his values.

Again, like sexual preferences, post-nup-based sanctions for political behaviors are unlikely to be upheld by a judge (e.g., "If he doesn't switch back to being a Democrat, he shouldn't be allowed joint custody"). But the biggest value of a post-nup for severe political conflicts is that it can set guidelines that limit or minimize this conflict. For instance, a post-nup might state that in the months leading up to a major election, there will be no dinner table conversation about politics. Setting some simple rules about politics—and formalizing them in a signed document—might take the edge off the conflict and help preserve the relationship.

- **Child raising.** We've touched on some of the disagreements about kids that can create marital tensions, such as the religion in which they're raised, blended families (and how much time a parent spends with stepkids versus children from former and current marriages), and the like. But other child-raising issues can exist that can create the same or more dissension. One of the most common ones is when one parent wants to homeschool a child and the other doesn't. Another could be when Dad wants to raise a child strictly (including corporal punishment) and Mom doesn't agree. Or a parent insists that her parents be involved in raising their kid and the other parent thinks her parents are a bad influence.

For another example, take a husband and wife who have a child with a serious medical condition. During the first five years after the child's birth, the husband and wife's arguments escalate over the quality and cost of the child's care. The husband maintains that the expensive private clinics and in-home nurses and therapists aren't worth the cost and that their child's quality of life will be the same if they choose less-expensive options. Through a post-nup, they negotiate a compromise and set a limit on how much they'll spend annually and on what treatments. In the case of a divorce, they also agree to adhere to these limits and who will pay what post-divorce (though, of course, judges always consider the best interest of the child in these decisions).

Unlike sex and politics, the courts take "best interest of the child" arguments seriously. For example, few courts would support strong corporal punishment. When Lois and Jack create a post-nup, they say that Lois cannot leave their children alone with her parents because when they drink, they become impatient with and at times physically abusive to the kids. If she ignores this agreement and drops the kids off with her parents, then if a divorce occurs, she will not ask for sole custody. When post-nups are structured like this so that a sanction is included for behavior that is counterproductive to a child, courts may uphold it.

Assess Your Marital Problems

Ask yourself the following questions to help identify which of the common problems are causing trouble in your marriage and how a post-nup might help solve them. Please remember that if the problems in your marriage are from an abusive situation, you should first seek the advice of an expert professional to assess your situation. A post-nup is not the right first step in abusive situations.

- **Do both you and your spouse express your feelings honestly and regularly?** Are you willing to risk embarrassment or even an angry argument in order to express how you really feel; are you willing to agree to attend couples counseling or set aside a specific amount of time weekly to focus on communication issues?

- **Do you and your spouse frequently disagree about financial matters or behaviors?** Is one of you a spendthrift while the other is frugal? Have you discovered that your spouse has made financial decisions of which you were unaware? Have your financial arguments increased in intensity and frequency over the course of your marriage?

- **Do you feel that your spouse is as committed to the marriage as you are?** Does he spend as much time with you and the kids as you would like? Does she seem to take the marriage for granted? Have either of you stopped being as involved emotionally as you once were?

- **Have your priorities changed over the course of your marriage?** Do you or your spouse have different objectives because of a midlife crisis, a family illness, or a career change? Have you ever tried to adjust your behaviors and those of your spouse so that you address these new priorities fairly and collaboratively?
- **Has your spouse been unfaithful?** Do you believe his affair is over and that he wants to make amends and never have an affair again? Would she be willing to sign an agreement that would demonstrate her commitment to you and her willingness to pay a penalty if she were to have another affair?
- **Have your or your spouse's expectations for the marriage changed during the time you've been married?** Have you discussed these changed expectations and how one or both of you are not getting your needs met?
- **Does your spouse frequently use drugs or drink too much?** Have these behaviors affected the marriage negatively? Have you tried to encourage your spouse to stop these behaviors, and he failed (even though he promises to stop)? Do you believe that she would be motivated to enter a rehab program or join a support group in order to cease these behaviors?
- **Do you and your spouse frequently engage in cyclical arguments about the same subjects?** Do you find that you're unable to resolve major issues, and instead keep going around and around in an increasingly frustrating manner? Would it help if you could be more creative in managing these conflicts by coming up with alternatives and compromises?

- **Do you and your spouse battle over sexual preferences, politics, or child raising?** Do you find yourself struggling to talk about sex honestly and openly? Are your arguments about politics heated? Can you think of any rules that might limit this conflict?

9

Dealing with Changes and Surprises

Lack of Mutual Assent, Misrepresentation, and Wild Cards

SOME MARITAL PROBLEMS can be traced back to the very inception of the marriage. Because they weren't dealt with effectively at the beginning, they simmer beneath the relationship's surface and at some point down the road, they emerge and threaten the marriage. Unlike many of the other marital issues we've discussed, these problems are rooted in the past. As difficult as it may be to deal with problems that arise later in the relationship—a spouse that starts drinking or has an affair—issues that are long-buried and long-ignored can be even more divisive when they arise.

Lack of mutual assent is one type of problem, and it suggests that couples have failed to come to an agreement about a major marital issue, such as whether they are going to have children. Sometimes, lack of mutual assent occurs because couples assume they are in agreement when they're not. For instance, John figures that Mary never wants to have children because she had a rough childhood. In fact, Mary does want to have kids but didn't discuss the topic with her husband; she just figures that they, like other couples they know, will start a family at some point. Five years down the road, however, when Mary finally does broach the subject, John tells her he assumed she didn't want kids. He feels he has too many work obligations now to consider fatherhood. Mary is shocked and eventually angered by his attitude, and her resentment that he never made his feelings known earlier eventually leads her to consider divorce.

Misrepresentation is related to mutual assent in that one person labors under a false assumption that existed from the beginning of the marriage. With misrepresentation, however, one spouse has misled his or her partner about some aspect of their history or behaviors. For instance, Steve doesn't tell Marcia that before they were married, he fathered a child and is secretly providing the mother with money to support that child. As you might imagine, when Marcia learns the truth about this earlier relationship five or ten years after they're married, she feels she can no longer trust her husband.

Wild cards refer to unexpected events and situations that arise later in a marriage—events and situations that neither spouse could anticipate when they were married. It could be a debilitating illness or a massive midlife crisis that causes a spouse to quit a good job and become a beekeeper. Whatever it is, this unexpected change wreaks havoc in a couple's life, and one spouse thinks back to the early days of the marriage and says to herself, "This isn't what I signed up for."

While these deeply rooted problems are not easily solved, post-nups provide couples with a forum to discuss them rationally and explore their options. Too often, there isn't an interim step between discovery of the lack of mutual assent, misrepresentation, or a wild card event and filing for divorce. Post-nups serve as a kind of fail-safe mechanism for the marriage, allowing couples to respond thoughtfully rather than reflexively to a problem from the past or an unanticipated life change in the present.

Lack of Mutual Assent: Types of Issues

If marriage operated like a business partnership, no one would say "I do" until all the potentially divisive issues were addressed in writing. Anticipated "what if" scenarios would be considered and specific responses to these scenarios would be spelled out and agreed to. Of course, it's not always easy to anticipate these scenarios. Perhaps more to the point, people might never get married if they had to hash out all the hot-button issues in advance of saying I do.

Instead, couples move forward and achieve clear consensus on some issues (living in a house rather than an apartment, having a dog or a cat, etc.) and only vague and sometimes incomplete or false assumptions on others. Here's a typical example of the latter. Harry and Sally discussed whether they would move from Seattle before they were married; both of them liked the city, had lots of friends and family nearby, and wanted to stay there. Harry, though, said that it was possible that at some point in the future a job opportunity might arise that might cause them to consider moving. Sally agreed that while this was a possibility in the future it was unlikely that Harry would receive such an offer in the next five years. Sally added that the odds were he would find a great job in Seattle, and that it was unlikely he would find something significantly better elsewhere. Harry agreed that she was probably right, and they both reaffirmed their desire to stay in Seattle.

Seven years later, Harry received an offer from a Dallas company that almost doubled his current salary. When he told Sally that they'd be crazy not to move and take this once-in-a-lifetime opportunity, Sally reminded him of their conversation about moving. She interpreted this earlier conversation to mean that they would stay in Seattle unless some extraordinary event took place. While she admitted the job offer was attractive, she said that Harry could use it as leverage to negotiate a salary increase at his current job. Harry, on the other hand, said he thought their earlier conversation meant that if he had the chance to make a lot more money, it would be a good reason to relocate. Both Sally and Harry became locked into their stances, and the argument escalated to the point that Sally threatened to divorce him if he took the job.

Lack of mutual assent can manifest itself in many different ways besides relocation: assumptions about how often they'll see certain friends and family members; how many children to have and how they'll be raised; the lifestyle they'll pursue and can afford; and so on. As you'll see, we often enter into marriage believing we're on the same page with regard to marital decisions and behaviors, while in fact there is a lack of mutual assent. Though it may not be a problem in the early years of the marriage, it can be a major divisive factor later on when couples have to make decisions about where to live, having children, and other lifestyle matters. As you'll discover, post-nups are tailor-made to address problems caused by lack of mutual assent. While some of these problems may be relatively trivial and unlikely to result in divorce (e.g., miscommunication about the type of vacations they'll take as a couple), others can have a significant impact on relationships.

Renegotiating the Problematic Issues

The odds are that couples talked about the assent issues that are causing problems at some point before or shortly after their marriage and negotiated a temporary truce. Many times, however, their conversations were incomplete or skirted the hot-button issues. Back then, the goal was to achieve a truce, not resolve deep-seated disagreements. Because the potential conflicts wouldn't become acute until months or years later, constructing a temporary if shallow agreement seemed preferable to having an all-out debate in the honeymoon stage.

Invariably, however, the issue comes to a head. When this happens, couples may end up in divorce shortly thereafter for two reasons:

- Poor communication
- A nonnegotiable position

In the former instance, couples get caught up in blaming and shaming rather than talking about the issue. They say things such as, "How is it possible that you didn't know I wanted to have children by age thirty?" and "It's your fault that we never discussed it if you feel so strongly about it!"

In the latter situation, one spouse is adamant, refusing to give an inch. He insists that despite everything she says about what they agreed to years ago, he will never move from their house. He is so dug into his point of view that he won't even consider any options.

Post-nups aren't used to assign blame since lack of mutual assent is no one's fault. Instead, they focus on the cause of the problem in the present (and in the future). It requires both spouses to explain their positions and provide substantive reasons for them. From there, they need to see if they can find middle ground or if one person is willing to move closer or accept the other person's position. The Action Pact can help people with nonnegotiable positions consider alternatives. For instance, Mary refuses to stay with Jim if he continues to spend like a drunken sailor and put the family's financial future in jeopardy. During the post-nup discussion, Jim says he is willing to spend money more responsibly but insists he is never going to be as frugal as Mary. In forging the Action Pact, Jim and Mary need to agree on actions that each will take in order to preserve the marriage. For Mary, her nonnegotiable is Jim's excessive spending. Therefore, one action that will appease her is if Jim takes a financial management class and agrees to adhere to a monthly spending limit—it may not be the ideal limit but it's in the ballpark and satisfies her nonnegotiable.

Misrepresentation: Breaking the Bond of Trust

While lack of mutual assent often is the innocent result of poor communication, misrepresentation is frequently the product of calculation. For instance, Tom doesn't tell Tanisha that he was married before and has two kids from that previous marriage out of fear that Tanisha won't marry him if she knows the truth. You may also misrepresent something from your past because you feel it's inconsequential or rationalize that it won't do any good telling your spouse—you don't inform him that you had an abortion when you were a teenager.

No matter what the motivation for the deceit is, when the other spouse finds out about it months or years later, this discovery creates distrust. This distrust eats away at the foundation of the marriage and can lead to divorce unless something is done—such as creating a post-nup.

Like lack of mutual assent, misrepresentation can take a variety of forms, including:

- **The desire to hide an event or behavior that causes shame.** A man doesn't want his wife to know that he received a suspended sentence for embezzlement, for instance.

- **A wish to spare a spouse the ugly truth.** In the Old South, gentlemen didn't disclose their tawdry behaviors to their wives because they wanted to spare them from the sordid facts. In the same way, someone may never speak of some unpleasant incident in his past, such as being caught up in a prostitution sting when he was in college.

- **A rationalization.** For example: "My spouse doesn't need to know that I was married and divorced and that my former wife in the court petition took out an order of protection against me. She was vindictive, so anything she might have accused me of has no relationship to the truth and it would just do a lot of harm if I were to tell my wife."

- **An intent to deceive.** In this case, one person believes that telling a lie will increase the odds that the other person will want to marry him. For instance, an individual may tell her intended that she is heir to a great fortune (when in reality it's a relatively small amount of money) or that he has an MBA from a prestigious university (when in fact he never finished his undergraduate degree).

Though many misrepresentations occur before a couple ties the knot, they can also crop up during the marriage. Hal is a business executive, and he sometimes takes direct reports with him to trade shows; in the last few years, his subordinate, Monique, has gone with him. Hal has never mentioned to his wife, Shirley, that anyone from his office attends trade shows with him. Therefore, when Shirley and Hal run into Monique at a restaurant a few days after his return from the trade show, Monique mentions something about the show and how valuable the experience was. Later, Shirley is furious with her husband for not disclosing that Monique accompanied him. Though Hal insists nothing untoward took place, Shirley maintains that he was lying by omission by not mentioning that Monique had accompanied him to the show for the past three years.

Once again, marriages should take a cue from the business world in forging agreements that govern the relationship. In business, contracts reflect the importance of avoiding any type of misrepresentations. In the sale of a business, a clause always exists in a contract that states a seller has not withheld relevant information about the business from the buyer and that he has disclosed any past or current problems.

In marriage, this same "full disclosure" mentality doesn't exist, which is especially problematic today for a number of reasons.

First, misrepresentations are much more likely to be discovered today than previously. E-mails, text messages, and social media ensure that secrets don't remain secrets for long; your spouse discovers e-mails from your former girlfriend whom you swore you would never communicate with again after you were married.

Second, more opportunities for misrepresentation exist than in the past. We live in an increasingly complex society where opportunities for bad behavior are rife. While growing gender equality in the workforce is a good thing, it also means that men and women work closely together—they work late, on weekends, and on trips together. As shown by our earlier example, even if nothing is going on, it's tempting to tell the white lie that you worked late by yourself or not mention that you were there with an attractive person half your age.

Third, financial stress can cause people to hide a variety of financial transactions from their spouse. You may be socking away a small amount every month for your kids' college education surreptitiously, fearing that your spouse will be angry if he learns you've been siphoning money away from immediate expenses. Or financial pressure may cause you to start day trading in an attempt to make more money. Or you may have a "secret" credit card that you use for purchases of which your spouse may disapprove because of their cost.

All this makes people misrepresent more—and get caught more! Fortunately, post-nups provide an alternative to the end of the marriage when your spouse becomes aware that you weren't completely honest.

Reestablishing Trust

One of the first things a post-nup does when misrepresentation has caused a marital rift is open the lines of communication. In many instances, misrepresentation can exist for years until it surfaces and causes problems. Those years of living a lie can make the misrepresentation difficult to discuss for both parties. As a result, the misrepresenter feels guilty and has trouble addressing his deception; the spouse who was deceived is so angry about being misled that she can't talk about the subject rationally.

The post-nup provides a focus for discussing this difficult subject as well as raising the possibility of divorce if the misrepresentation and its consequences aren't addressed. Many times, the communication dam-breaker is identifying why an individual misrepresented the truth. It may be that Jerry never told his wife, Julie, about his previous marriage because he was embarrassed by it—he felt like he was young and stupid and made a choice that was a colossal blunder. When Julie discovered that Jerry was married before (she learned about the marriage when she cleaned out some boxes in the attic and found a letter from Jerry's ex-wife), she assumed that Jerry never told her because he still had feelings for his former wife. It was only when they had their post-nup discussion that she understood why Jerry never told her about his first marriage and was able to consider forgiving him.

The post-nup also specifies consequences for the misrepresenting spouse if he doesn't come clean or fails to practice full disclosure regarding other matters. Again, the post-nup helps preserve the marriage because the offending spouse is motivated to behave better. But in the case of misrepresentation, it also helps to re-establish trust in the relationship. In discussing the new terms of the relationship, couples are testing whether they can trust each other. Is the offending spouse willing to agree to a no-secrets policy? Are both spouses able to compromise sufficiently that neither feels the need to withhold information or lie about behaviors? After the post-nup is put into practice, couples assess their ability to be honest with each other, to be transparent, to talk about difficult issues. If they can do so effectively, they start restoring relationship trust.

In creating post-nup language for misrepresentation issues, be careful about not overreacting. If the consequences are too severe and the behavioral restrictions too harsh, the post-nup can cause the offending party to opt for divorce. One way of avoiding overreacting is to have a series of discussions about the misrepresentation and its consequences, and then allowing days or weeks to pass between discussions. In this way, you give yourself time to think about what's fair and effective, as well as terms with which you wouldn't be comfortable.

You should also pose "what if" scenarios. For instance: "What if my boss has me take out our assistant for lunch to celebrate her three-year anniversary with the firm? I know I said I'd disclose any time I spend alone with young, single women, but would you consider this a violation of the post-nup if I didn't tell you about it?" These "what if" scenarios will help you establish fair terms, identifying what should be disclosed and what is inconsequential.

In addition, you can use the post-nup to determine areas that neither of you has to disclose. Some issues may be too painful to discuss, or you may recognize that a discussion at this point will be counterproductive. For instance, you agree not to say anything when an old boyfriend or girlfriend contacts you through social media. While you may agree to disclose any phone calls or personal meetings with these individuals, one-time, brief online contact may not be sufficient to require disclosure. If you both are aware that the mention of this contact can create an angry, potentially relationship-damaging fight, you may decide to allow nondisclosure in these situations.

Wild Cards

Life deals couples wild cards, and most people aren't prepared for them. More to the point, these wild cards affect the assumptions upon which the marriage was originally founded. Will and Martha married seven years ago, and they both were united in their belief that they should live as simply as possible. As a result, they moved to a rural area, raising much of their own food and making just enough to survive. When they had two children a few years into the marriage, Will supplemented their income by doing handyman jobs in the area. They managed to scrape by, but they were under increasing financial stress that translated into emotional stress, especially for Will.

Then out of the blue, Martha inherited close to half a million dollars when her grandmother passed away. Martha wanted to put the money in trust funds for their children while maintaining their current lifestyle, but Will was adamant that they needed to make changes, such as moving to a bigger, nicer house in an area with better schools than their rural community offered. Will was also tired of living so simply. He told Martha he didn't want anything extravagant, just a car that wasn't constantly breaking down and cable television.

Martha was shocked and told Will so. She said they had ideals and were living an idyllic life. How could he have changed so much? Why was he so greedy? Their arguments escalated, and soon they were on the verge of a divorce.

Wild cards come in many shapes and sizes, but they usually affect the relationship dynamic in a significant way. Typically, one person responds to the wild card event by wanting things to change, and the other person resists this change. Here are three typical wild card events:

- **A major shift in financial circumstances** (either positive or negative), such as a spouse losing a job, windfall profits from an investment, etc. In a positive scenario, one spouse wants a major lifestyle change—moving to a bigger house in a nicer neighborhood, making other major purchases, and so on. In the negative situation, one spouse insists that the other get a job or that they sell their residence and move somewhere cheaper.

- **A health crisis.** The spouse or children develop a serious illness or a loved one becomes sick and requires one spouse's care. This can place emotional and financial strain on the relationship. For instance, one spouse spends every weekend caring for her ailing parent.
- **A sea change in beliefs or interests.** For example, a nonreligious spouse becomes a born-again Christian; or a politically liberal person becomes an arch-conservative; or a middle class businessperson decides he wants to chuck their bourgeois lifestyle and move to a developing nation where they can fight hunger and poverty. A particular event can trigger these changes—a near-death experience, a midlife crisis—or they might just arise from a series of circumstances. Whatever the cause, one person in the relationship experiences a major life transformation while his partner does not. This creates tension that can harm the relationship.

While wild cards can destroy marriages, post-nups can save them. Part of the problem of a wild card is that it changes the marital bargain in a way that is unacceptable to one spouse. Too often, it causes couples to repeat the same argument about this change until one or both of the spouses can't stand it any longer and divorce happens. A post-nup recasts the nature of the argument, and ideally it recasts it for the better.

First, it demonstrates how serious the situation has become—it's not just another marital argument but one that very possibly could have divorce as a consequence. It disabuses the spouse who has initiated the change as to his spouse's ability to adapt to the new circumstances; contrary to what he had hoped, she is not willing to become a Buddhist or live in India.

Second, it forces the couple to examine their own values and preferences and whether they jibe with the changed situation. For instance, are the spouses able to tolerate a role reversal, where Dad becomes the homemaker and Mom becomes the breadwinner?

Third, it gives a couple the opportunity to hammer out a compromise. To avoid divorce, how willing are you to moderate the changed circumstances that are endangering the marriage? To avoid divorce, how willing are you to accept some of the changed circumstances that your spouse has caused or embraced?

Fourth, it requires you to work out an action plan on paper. To adapt to change, couples need to commit to definitive actions within a definitive time frame: John has to agree to find a caregiver for his ailing mom so he spends more time with the family, and Mary has to agree to stop criticizing John for prioritizing his mother over his own family; and they need to take these actions within a three-month period and monitor their ability to live up to their commitments.

Assess Your Changes and Wild Cards

Review the following questions to determine if lack of mutual assent, misrepresentation, or wild cards are causing problems in your marriage and how a post-nup might help you deal with these problems.

- **Is there a significant marital issue that you assume you'd reach agreement on but it turns out that you have not?**
- **Is the lack of mutual assent related to money, alcohol or drugs, children, or friends and family?**
- **Is the lack of mutual assent caused by poor communication?**

This could be from early on in your relationship up until the point the problem surfaces. Is it caused by one spouse taking a nonnegotiable position on the issue? Are you focusing your post-nup discussion on finding a way to resolve this specific roadblock?

- **How has misrepresentation manifested itself in your marriage?** Is it related to one spouse hiding a shameful behavior? Was it an attempt to shield a spouse from an ugly truth? Was there a self-justifying rationalization or an attempt to deceive?

- **Is your post-nup discussion aimed at re-establishing trust that has been broken because of the misrepresentation?** Are you posing "what if" scenarios in an attempt to find trust-building behaviors that both spouses are comfortable with?

- **Has a wild card event or circumstances created a rift between you and your spouse?** Does this wild card involve a positive or negative event that affects your finances? Does it have to do with a serious health problem? Does it revolve around one spouse's new beliefs or interests?

- **Are you using the post-nup to create thought and discussion about how you both are reacting to this change?** Does the post-nup discussion address whether you can tolerate a given change to the marital contract? If so, are you creating an Action Pact that specifies what each of you must do and when in order to accommodate the life-changing event or circumstance?

10

Special Situations

Blended Families, Nontraditional Partnerships, High Net Worth, and More

THE FLEXIBILITY OF POST-NUPS is part of what makes them so useful, since marital problems are tremendously varied. You can completely shape your post-nup to serve your particular purpose. As a contract, post-nups require "offer, acceptance, and consideration." If these legal criteria are met—if you both enter into the contract freely and knowledgeably—then you and your spouse can agree to just about anything as long as you both have equal bargaining positions and aren't violating any laws.

Though we've discussed a variety of situations where post-nups might apply, we've just scratched the surface. Marriages as well as relationships are far more complex than in the past and are becoming even more complicated. As a result, the situations that pose challenges to couples are more diverse than ever before.

Consider the changes in society that raised all sorts of new issues for couples:

- Increasing number of blended families

- Legalization of gay marriage
- Medical advances (e.g., sperm donors)
- Changes in adoption laws
- The use of prenups
- The spread of social media

As a result of these and other changes in social norms, science and technology, and law, couples are struggling with issues that were rare or nonexistent as little as ten or twenty years ago. Too often, their marriages are endangered because they lack an effective tool to deal with the conflicts these changes produce. Post-nups can be tailored to help manage their conflicts, no matter how unusual they might be.

The Range of Situations

As you might imagine, the relative newness and diversity of situations can bedevil judges when couples are divorcing. They often must make decisions without the benefit of an established body of law to guide them. More to the point, they are often called upon to issue decisions in politically sensitive areas—gay and lesbian rights, religion (e.g., blended families with different spousal religions), and so on. Remember that judges are often elected officials. They would much prefer to say that they made a decision based on what two people agreed to in a post-nup rather than on their own interpretation of sketchy legal precedents.

To understand how difficult these problems are for both the courts and the individuals involved—and how a post-nup might resolve them before they reach the divorce stage—let's look at some relatively new relationship complexities.

A couple discovers they can't have children, and one spouse wants to adopt a child from a foreign country (something that was not a possibility twenty years ago) and the other doesn't. This disagreement threatens to tear the marriage apart, but a post-nup provides a way to satisfy both spouses' requirements. The spouse that initially didn't want to adopt feared that her spouse wasn't thinking through all the medical and social issues. She feared that his desire to adopt any child at any age might result in them taking in a child with issues they were not prepared to handle as parents. So she agrees in a post-nup to adoption, but only if they provide the adoption agency with certain guidelines: a baby under six months of age, in good health, from an American family with no family history of drug or alcohol abuse.

Another couple weds and has three children. The marriage is fine for the first ten years, but then the wife has an affair with another woman. The affair ends, but the husband suspects that his wife is a lesbian, even though she won't admit it—she comes from a conservative background and has trouble accepting the possibility of being gay. She vows never to have an affair again, but her husband is convinced that eventually she'll come to accept her identity and that the marriage will end. If that happens, he wants to be sure that he, his wife, and the kids go through therapy with a counselor trained in transitioning families to same-sex relationships. So they create a post-nup that stipulates that in the event that the wife leaves him for a woman, the family will undergo counseling for a period of at least six months and longer if the therapist feels it's necessary.

As the population ages, we're bound to see more divorces among couples who have been married for thirty or more years, and this will make post-nups even more important. Some of the divorces will happen because of retirement—the couple functioned well when one or both of the spouses were at work, but now that they're both retired, they get on each other's nerves to the point that the marriage is tension-filled and headed for divorce court. In anticipation of these problems, aging couples can create post-nups that make it easier both for them and for judges to create a fair distribution of assets.

After thirty or forty years, couples accumulate a lot of stuff—and a lot of psychological baggage. Having an agreement in place helps avoid acrimonious, stress-inducing, and costly divorces for couples in their senior years—the last thing you want when you're sixty-five, have a heart condition, and are trying to make sure you have enough money for a secure retirement.

So post-nups aren't just for couples in their thirties and forties. In fact, we're likely to see more seniors considering ending their relationships for a variety of reasons. For instance, Joe and Tina were married for thirty-five years; Joe was a highly successful partner in an architectural firm who routinely worked sixty-hour weeks. Though they experienced some rough patches throughout the marriage—at one point they had a trial separation—they hung in there, as much for their kids as for themselves. After thirty-three years, though, the marital situation changed. Tina was diagnosed as having lupus. Joe began working from home so that he could help take care of her. For Tina, though, the disease was a wake-up call. It caused her to reevaluate everything in her life, including her marriage—she had found herself becoming increasingly alienated from Joe's obsession with work and neglect of her needs. When her doctors found a drug regimen that helped stabilize her condition, she decided she wanted to make a fresh start and filed for divorce. It was a complex, difficult divorce, in large part because Joe was blindsided by it and resentful and angry because of all the sacrifices he had made to help his wife. Though they weathered the storms of their marriage before Tina was diagnosed, they might have weathered them better if they confronted the behaviors that were driving them apart. If they had created a post-nup after their trial separation, for instance, they could have at least reached agreement on division of their assets. At best, they might have been able to address Tina's unarticulated dissatisfaction with her life; they might have included an Action Pact clause motivating Joe to stop paying so much attention to work and so little attention to Tina.

Our aging population is far more independent-minded and less concerned about tradition than previous generations. As a result, they are more likely to consider divorce even if they have been married for a long period of time. Senior divorce, then, is another special situation that post-nups can help address.

Let's take a close-up look at three particular special situations and how post-nups should be used to deal with these issues.

Blended Families

Though we've covered some of the marital problems that arise with blended families and how post-nups can help, we've just scratched the surface. When couples bring children from previous relationships to a new marriage, tension points are almost always present, and they can take many different forms. Even more problematic, these tension points are often ignored or downplayed early on in the marriage. It's difficult to foresee an argument about the religion a child will be raised in when he's a toddler or a conflict over how much money will be spent on a young child's college education.

For instance, Ernie and Carol are married and have two adolescent children, but Ernie has a daughter, Lexi, from a previous marriage. Lexi is twenty-three and recently graduated from college with a degree in art. She wants to pursue her dream of becoming a professional artist—she's an abstract painter—and Ernie is encouraging her to do so. He says he will help pay her rent and other expenses as she attempts to establish herself as an artist. Carol is furious at Ernie, saying that you have to work for everything you get. Unlike Ernie, who grew up in an upper middle class family, Carol has a blue-collar background. From her perspective, supporting Lexi is not only bad from a life philosophy basis, but it will also require them to divert money away from savings for their two adolescent children's college educations.

What's more important, Carol asks Ernie: subsidizing his adult child or helping their own two kids go to college?

This isn't really a fair question, but it's the type of question that they should have considered earlier in their marriage. Now it has created a lot of tension, but they can address that by creating a post-nup to hammer out a compromise. Perhaps Ernie suggests that he pay only for a certain percentage of Lexi's expenses, or that they devote X percent of his income to saving for their other children's educations. Carol can express her belief in the importance of kids making it on their own once they leave the nest. She and Ernie will discuss what level of support is acceptable for Lexi, then create consequences for violating their agreement, motivating both of them to adhere to the post-nup's terms.

In blended families, all sorts of philosophical and financial conflicts arise, and they can threaten the marriage if they are allowed to fester. As the previous example illustrated, spouses often have different child-raising philosophies—one believes in giving kids everything, another believes in raising children to be self-reliant. While these differing beliefs can cause conflict in any marriage, they are particularly divisive forces in blended families. Typically, one spouse accuses the other of "treating *your* child better than *our* child."

These accusations often are triggered by the college selection process. For instance, a couple has three children: one from the husband's previous marriage, one from the wife's previous marriage, and one together. The wife's daughter is attending an expensive, elite private university; the husband's son is going to a less expensive state school. Their third child is a junior in high school, and the husband and wife start having huge arguments about where he can and should apply. The frugal husband insists that "a state university was good enough for me and John [his son from the previous marriage], so it's good enough for Carl." His wife believes that their son's excellent grades and academic interests should be rewarded by paying for him to go to an elite university. The argument is exacerbated by the philosophies they followed with their older kids from previous marriages. The precedents have been set, and they feel it would be unfair to break with them: that the husband's older son would resent it if he had to go to a state school and their younger son is allowed to attend a private one and that their younger son would resent it if his older stepsister goes to a private school and he's denied that privilege.

By using a post-nup as a launching point for discussing these issues, a great deal of acrimony can be avoided. Guidelines are set at a time when tensions don't run high (ideally, before the children enter high school), so the discussion is rational and compromise is possible. These guidelines are also valuable in the event that a couple divorces. Some courts rule that when it comes to a child's college education, one spouse pays a third, the other spouse pays a third, and the child is responsible for one third (via loans, work, etc.). But if a couple doesn't feel this formula is right for them, they can work out a more equitable payment division in a post-nup, and the court is likely to adhere to this agreement (unless, of course, it's egregious in some way—e.g., the couple insists that the child is responsible for the entire college tuition).

Same-Sex Marriages and Long-Term Partners

Whether you are gay and living as a couple without marriage or straight and ABM (All But Married), you are in a special legal situation because so little case law exists to govern your relationship. Even gay couples who marry are in special situations because they may face issues for which there is little legal precedent. A post-nup, therefore, offers couples legal protections that they may not otherwise have, and it also helps judges make decisions in divorce or relationship-ending cases.

Increasingly, states are leaning toward granting marital rights to couples who have lived together for a significant period of time. Given this trend, it stands to reason that the courts will honor legally viable post-nups for non-married couples as they would for married partners. Colorado, for instance, is one of these states, and I recently wrote a post-nup for a Colorado couple who had never married but had a child and had been together for a number of years.

This shift can be seen in Illinois's Cook County court system. For decades, paternity cases were considered in separate courts from those in which divorce and family-type issues were adjudicated. In 2017, paternity cases began to be heard in the same courts as divorces.

On a related front, more young people than ever before are living together—and having children together—without getting married. This trend among millennials can create havoc later on if they decide to split up. Many times, besides having children, they also buy property together and accumulate other expensive goods. Yet when they break up, the law will treat them as strangers. She may say to the judge, "I know only his name is on the property deed, but he always told me that it was my house as much as his" or "We had an agreement that I would stay home and take care of the house and our child and he'd work, and that he'd always take care of us financially no matter what." Yet all these promises are made outside of a legally binding relationship, and so the courts may ignore them. While a state like California has dealt with some of these issues in palimony cases involving movie stars, most states have not recognized these relationships in their rulings or held that unmarried partners enjoy the same rights as married ones.

So post-nups can provide these couples with legal protection as they facilitate conflict resolution. Without a legally binding marital contract, these relationships are inherently fragile. People act impulsively, and couples living together can break up more easily when they get in fights because, both legally and psychologically, they are not part of legally validated relationship. With a post-nup, however, they have an interim, legally valid step between an argument and a break-up. They can use this document to discuss and negotiate options and compromises that might help the relationship over the rough patches. And further, the law will recognize bona fide contracts, which the post-nup should be. Courts may not recognize informal oral agreements, especially when the parties hate each other and contest whether any oral agreements ever existed. The post-nup creates a formal, legal agreement.

High Net Worth Partnerships

In chapter 6, we discussed how Property Pacts are used in post-nups when you possess significant assets. This was probably relevant to many of you, since after a number of years of marriage and work, you've probably accumulated a lot of stuff, even if you don't think of yourself as wealthy. Here, though, I want to look at post-nups specifically from the perspective of high net worth individuals.

If you happen to have a lot of money, then it may seem like you don't need a post-nup since there will be plenty of dollars to go around if you get divorced. But high net worth couples are in a special situation because all that money creates complexity, and that complexity can in turn produce a great deal of stress if the marriage starts falling apart.

Take the case of Chicago billionaire hedge fund manager Ken Griffin and his wife, Anne. In 2014, the couple filed for divorce, and they began fighting a war of accusations and cross-accusations through their lawyers and the media. For instance, one media story revolved around Ken Griffin's claim that his wife was amassing $1 million in monthly expenses for everything from dining to vacations to a private jet. She in turn accused her husband of taking advantage of her anxiety and intimidating her into signing a prenup. The legal battle dragged on for over a year, and the disagreements were not only about money but about Anne relocating to New York from Chicago with the children. This case finally settled on the verge of trial.

The entire situation seems nightmarish, creating animosity between the spouses and enormous legal bills. On top of that, the hostile, dragged-out divorce process is certainly not in the best interest of the children.

If the couple had a post-nup in place, they may have avoided this nightmare by including the following in such a document:

- Full disclosure of all assets
- Agreement about how these assets would be divided if they were to divorce
- A statement from both spouses about how much money they would each need to maintain an acceptable lifestyle
- An agreement about custody arrangements, visitation, and maintenance and support payments

While the Griffins had a prenup and the case settled, these agreements can be a dicey proposition for judges, especially when situations change dramatically during the course of a relationship. For instance, let's say two young techies who are writing code and dreaming of creating an app get married. Though they are far from wealthy early on in the marriage, the husband is a little older than his wife and has managed to accumulate a small condo and some savings. His wife immediately agrees to his request for a prenup, since she's giving up very little by signing it. Ten years later when she files for divorce, though, their startup is worth $500 million. Though her husband is the president and CEO, she has been instrumental in its success, even though she lacks an official title. The prenup, though, denies her a fair share of the company. Judges generally enforce prenups, but the disadvantaged spouse will seek to have it thrown out in these situations, since a couple's financial realities when they signed it have changed in major ways. In addition, the person who is disadvantaged by the prenup can also make the argument that her spouse pressured her to sign. This same argument can't be made with a post-nup.

Finally, if you're a high net worth couple and you decide to do a post-nup, videotape the agreement to avoid future challenges. While this is good advice no matter what your financial circumstances may be, it's especially relevant for well-to-do couples. A video of the signing of the post-nup will seal the deal in many instances. Judges are more confident in enforcing agreements couples forge when it's backed up with video that reinforces the terms in the post-nup—it provides additional proof that the agreement was entered into freely by both parties. Of course, consult your lawyer regarding the advisability of videotaping your post-nup.

Assess Your Special Situations

To determine if post-nups apply to your particular circumstances— if they can help you resolve the conflicts that beset your marriage or achieve a "good" divorce if you can't—consider the following questions.

> • **If you were to get divorced, would a judge struggle to find legal precedent with which to making a ruling in your case?** Are you or your spouse likely to be disadvantaged financially or in other ways upon divorce because of your relationship status?

- **Were you or your spouse previously married and do one or both of you have kids from your previous marriages?** Do you also have children in your current marriage? Do you anticipate having escalating arguments about what's fair for "your" children versus your spouse's children from former relationships?

- **Are you in a long-term relationship that is not a legally sanctioned marriage?** Have you considered the negative impact if you were to break up in terms of division of your combined assets, health insurance, and other issues?

- **Are you an unmarried gay or straight couple?** Have you ever discussed who gets what if you were to break up? Do you have a verbal agreement about how your property will be divided or how custody and maintenance issues will be addressed? Thinking about a worst-case scenario, do you think you and your partner might argue about any of these issues if you were to break up?

- **Are you a high net worth couple?** Do you own a large amount of property, have numerous and varied investments, and other valuable assets? Do you have a prenup that you signed many years ago? If you were to divorce, do you anticipate that you and your spouse may disagree about the division of assets, maintenance, and custody? Can you foresee yourself or your spouse using the media to try your case in the public eye?

11

The Post-Nup Attorney

How to Maximize a Lawyer's Value

WHILE YOU DON'T NEED A LAWYER to create a post-nup in the same way you need a lawyer to file for divorce, consulting one is a good idea. Some couples can write rough drafts of their post-nups, especially if the issues aren't overly complex and they agree on the key provisions. In addition, when the post-nup helps a spouse change offending behaviors and the marriage gets back on track, no litigation is necessary.

But the involvement of attorneys can increase the odds that a post-nup will benefit a couple. First, if the post-nup fails to save the marriage, this involvement can lessen the cost and stress of a divorce, as well as make a fair settlement more likely. Over the years, I've represented thousands of clients in various areas of the law, and every so often clients suggest that they would like to write a contract or some other legal document. They may even do a reasonably good job—for laypeople. And that's the issue. Without legal training, couples are likely to make mistakes in how they word these documents. When they become the object of litigation, a few wrong words can make a huge difference—the difference between winning and losing a case, as well as a significant amount of money. Therefore, when laypeople show me the documents they have written, I invariably have to rewrite them so they contain enforceable language.

Second, attorneys can facilitate the use of a post-nup to increase communication and change behaviors within a marriage. A good divorce attorney will possess the experience and expertise to help craft a post-nup that is realistic rather than idealistic. For instance, a couple might decide to do a post-nup in which a spouse has to engage in a family activity each weekend; if he misses two such activities, a divorce will ensue. If such conduct would be enforced in your state, an attorney might suggest a "sunset provision" as part of the post-nup—if the spouse adheres to this requirement for one year, then the provision is dropped from the post-nup. Such a suggestion may help avoid creating resentment on the part of the bad-behaving spouse, who had been on his best behavior and starts to feel like the provision is unfair, given this changed behavior. The sunset provision is just one of many techniques divorce attorneys possess that can help foster a better post-nup.

If you work with an attorney on your post-nup, though, you need to know how to choose the right one and ensure he or she provides the counsel and renders the services that will help you achieve your objectives—ideally as a couple, but not so ideally as a divorcing individual.

Selection: How to Find the Best Attorney for Your Needs

Not every lawyer can do a post-nup. To help find the most qualified person with the right knowledge and attitude necessary, here are three criteria for hiring a post-nup attorney.

- **Find an attorney who specializes in divorce/family law.** Because a post-nup has similarities to a business partnership contract—and because you and your spouse may have a relatively simple agreement—you may think that a business attorney or any generalist can do a good job. While there may be a place for a business attorney in the post-nup-creation process (for instance, when one spouse has his own business), divorce attorneys know the territory. Not only do they know the laws in your state regarding maintenance, custody, and so on but they know the judges—they can assess a given judge's receptivity to this type of agreement.

- **Look for a lawyer who is aware of the post-nup concept or has a positive attitude toward it.** You're going to encounter attorneys who scoff at post-nups. Some do so because they are traditionalists and believe in the tried-and-true divorce process. A small minority might dislike the idea because post-nups represent a loss of income for them (they will receive far more money representing a client in a divorce than in handling a post-nup), but despite the media's cynical portrayals of lawyers, few make decisions out of personal self-interest. While you may not find a lawyer who has done a lot of post-nups, you should search for one who is open to the idea and willing to follow your lead.

- **Use a lawyer's flexibility as a litmus test.** Is a lawyer willing to let you and your spouse draft the post-nup and then review it to make sure the language is right? Is the lawyer willing to take you on as a client even though your spouse lacks representation? Is the attorney amenable to language in the post-nup about conduct? Is the attorney willing to work with a therapist or other counselor to help create an effective post-nup? Flexibility is critical because post-nups work best when they're tailored to a specific marital situation. Your attorney should be willing to include clauses that he may never have included in a standard divorce settlement, to be creative in structuring the agreement so it meets your requirements as a couple.

Beyond these criteria, another key to the selection process is relying on attorneys you know or work with for a referral. If you have a business attorney, for instance, ask him if he knows a divorce attorney who might meet the previous three criteria. Attorneys are often plugged into the legal grapevine; they may not specialize in divorce, but they have colleagues who are skilled in this area. Relying on referrals is better than picking a name from an online listing or responding to an ad.

Be prepared to shop around. Lawyers by nature are conservative creatures. When you talk to them about wanting to do a post-nuptial agreement, they may shake their head and tell you that they're not sure if it's enforceable. They may agree to take you on as a client only if you sign a letter agreeing that they've advised you that a post-nup may not be enforceable.

Don't be dissuaded by this last requirement. As long as the lawyer agrees to prepare a post-nup and to include language that encourages a judge to enforce it, this attorney should do a good job for you.

Still, be aware that you may have to visit more than one attorney before you find one who is savvy about post-nups or at least amenable to trying to help you create one.

At the same time, don't assume that a divorce attorney who has done a lot of prenups will be willing and able to do post-nups. Prenups are about property exclusively. Post-nups are about conduct and property. They may be loath to cross the line and deal with something as "messy" as conduct, preferring the relatively cut-and-dried matters of residential properties, retirement accounts, and the like. Yes, these attorneys may have a good grasp of what a nuptial agreement entails, but the issues involved in pre- and post- are night and day.

You should also expect a range of estimated fees for service, but by and large, they should be significantly lower than what you would pay for an average divorce. In fact, if you just need an attorney to review a simple post-nup that you and your spouse drafted, the cost could be as little as $1,500. A divorce in a major city costs a minimum of $10,000 and can quickly escalate to $100,000 or more. Whatever you pay for work on your post-nup, look at it as a cost-effective estimate. If it helps you avoid a divorce, then you've saved not only your marriage but also whatever a divorce would cost you. But even if the post-nup doesn't prevent a divorce, it still can help you save money. The legal fees will be less because the post-nup agreement is in place, resulting in less time spent by the lawyer and less contention during the divorce process (disagreements usually result in a lot more work for the lawyer and cost for the client).

What Your Lawyer Needs to Know, and What You Can Expect

Once you select your lawyer, you need to communicate the following in your first working meeting:

- That you want to do a post-nup and why
- What you want to include in the agreement
- What you want the attorney to do (versus what you want to do)

This sounds simple, but in reality, it can be a bit more complicated, in part because your attorney may never have done a post-nup before. Therefore, you need to be clear from the start and explain your perception of a post-nup and why you want to do one. For instance, you might start out telling your lawyer something along these lines:

"I've been married for twelve years, and I have issues in my marriage—I'm concerned because my spouse had an affair last year and even though he ended it, I won't tolerate this behavior again. We've talked about this issue, but talking isn't enough because there are no consequences if he cheats again—I'll get upset, we'll have a big fight, then he'll promise never to do it again and things will settle down . . . until the next time. So I've read about post-nuptial agreements, and what I like is they provide negative consequences for spousal bad behavior.

"I also know my spouse, and that if I file for divorce now, it will be World War III. We'll never have a chance for a normal relationship, and I think we still might have a chance. So I'd like to give it one more try with a post-nup, but I also want to set up an agreement where we address what happens if we divorce, who gets what. I know my spouse will be a lot more reasonable about divvying up everything fairly at this point while we're still trying to make the relationship work."

Next, you'll get into the specifics of what you want the post-nup to say. You and your spouse have already written up an agreement, or you may want your lawyer to write something based on your key points. In either case, the critical aspect of the post-nup is the behavior clause with a trigger—you want your spouse to stop having affairs and start going to therapy with you, and if he can't maintain these new behaviors, a divorce will ensue with negative sanctions as a result. Your lawyer needs to know exactly what you're proposing so she can advise you about the enforceability of this behavioral stipulation.

Ideally, your attorney will proceed to create the post-nup or amend the one you've created, but be prepared for some attorneys to express skepticism that your spouse will sign it. They may say something like, "Your spouse would have to be an idiot to sign something like this." Earlier, I suggested that you need to look for a lawyer who is positive about the idea of a post-nup, but it's possible that they weren't being honest about their views during the screening process—they just wanted to get you in their office in the hopes of representing you in a conventional divorce. If this is the case, walk away and find a new lawyer.

The majority of attorneys will be positive and do what you request, but they still may have one caveat. In Illinois and many other states, an attorney can create a post-nup for both of you, but he can only represent one of you. The unrepresented spouse can either retain her own counsel or sign a document agreeing to be unrepresented. So even though you and your spouse may have created a post-nup yourself and be in agreement on all the issues, be prepared for your attorney to advise the unrepresented spouse to obtain counsel. This is a fundamental principle of family law—each side has representation. Your attorney's reflex will probably be to recommend that you both have different lawyers. Yes, this increases your expenses a bit, but it usually is a good precaution. Even if you're in agreement about the post-nup and its provisions, it makes psychological sense for both of you to be represented. This way, neither of you will feel that the legal document is biased in favor of one of you because "your" attorney helped create it. The judge is likely to feel the same way.

What services will attorneys provide to facilitate the post-nup process? Here are some of the ways attorneys help increase the enforceability and effectiveness of these legal documents.

• **Review or write an existing post-nup to ensure it conforms to state law.** As you might imagine, couples include all sorts of behavioral clauses in a post-nup that reflect the wide range of problems in a marriage. Sometimes, though, one spouse will put in a clause that represents "punishment" or is requesting the court to do something that violates the law. For instance, one spouse wants a clause that says if her spouse starts drinking again, he will never be allowed to see his children for the rest of his life. An attorney can suggest other alternatives that will be legally viable and also are more likely to result in a change in marital behavior.

- **Unravel the complexities.** Just as marital relationships can be complex, post-nups too can involve myriad issues. It may be that a couple wants to create behavioral clauses for each other (rather than just one spouse, which is simpler). It may be that the provisions in the post-nup affect not only a couple's children but kids from previous marriages. It may be that the couple is wealthy and the post-nup has to deal with lots of assets. Lawyers are skilled at creating legal documents that address complex subjects. They are experienced at creating contracts (and a post-nup is a variation on a business contract) that are legally viable and resolve difficult conflicts to the satisfaction of all parties.

- **Amend the post-nup over time.** Earlier, I stressed the importance of keeping post-nups up to date. While couples can do this on their own, attorneys are skilled about how to change the language or add provisions that don't just reflect changing situations but increase the odds that the post-nup will still be enforceable if a divorce occurs. Remember, an attorney understands contracts and knows how to update them so they reflect new realities. For instance, let's say John and Mary have a sixteen-year-old stepson, Tim, from Mary's previous marriage. A major source of friction in the marriage is that John is dismissive toward Tim. Their post-nup includes a provision that dictates John attend regular family counseling sessions with Mary and Tim to deal with his hostility toward his stepson. But when Tim reaches the age of eighteen and leaves home to go to college, the situation changes and the post-nup needs to be amended. An attorney may suggest a different behavioral clause for John—instead of group counseling, he may switch to less frequent individual therapy. Similarly, a post-nup may revolve around a spouse's out-of-control spending habits; the provision in the post-nup states that this spouse cannot use a credit card or make a significant purchase without prior approval from her spouse. But to have this provision in place indefinitely may start to feel overly punitive to the spendthrift spouse, especially if she limits her spending for a period of time. The attorney may suggest a "sunset" clause in which after one year of good spending behavior, the attorney and the couple review the situation and, if everyone agrees, either modify or eliminate this clause.

When the Post-Nup Turns into Divorce

Let's say your spouse violates the post-nup agreement; he has agreed to stop gambling but you have evidence that he's started again. Your post-nup states in the event of a divorce, he will forfeit his right to the couple's jointly owned artwork (which he values) and that he will have to pay back all the money he lost gambling in the five years after the divorce is final.

At this point, a good lawyer will ask you if you really want to activate the divorce provisions in the post-nup. Just because you have a document that entitles you to file for divorce because of your spouse's behavior doesn't mean it's the right thing to do. For instance, in this example, it may be that your spouse started gambling again because he was under a lot of pressure at work, his best friend died in an accident, and so on. In other words, the circumstances were unusual, and he slipped up.

Your lawyer should not have a knee-jerk reaction and file for divorce without discussing the issue with you. More specifically, your attorney should say something like, "Do you feel that this violation merits filing for divorce? Or do you feel that there is something we can do within the confines of the post-nup to address this behavior, perhaps an amendment that will address this recent problem?"

A savvy attorney will also talk with you about violations of the letter of the "law" versus the spirit in which the trigger clause was written. Perhaps your spouse was in Nevada on a business trip and confesses to you that he spent twenty bucks gambling on the slots in the airport because he was bored. While this *is* a violation of the post-nup, it is a relatively minor one: he limited his gambling to a small amount of money and time and he admitted to the violation right after it occurred. He also promised it wouldn't happen again. Attorneys aren't traffic cops, issuing tickets for violations and not listening to any excuse. They should help you achieve the outcome that is best for you, and to do that they should help you explore your options rather than acting as if your only option is divorce.

Let's say you decide that divorce is what you want—it wasn't $20 on airport slots, it was $20,000 at the blackjack tables—and that you want the terms of the post-nup enforced. What's to prevent your spouse from challenging those terms in the same way that some people challenge prenups? Might he claim that he was "coerced" into signing the post-nup, insisting that you blackmailed him by threatening to file for divorce unless he agreed to the terms?

In the majority of cases, this claim of coercion will be ignored by the courts. In some prenups, an older, wealthy man insists his younger, less wealthy spouse-to-be sign the document almost immediately before the marriage and imposes terms that are heavily weighted in his favor; the presumption is, if she doesn't sign, there will be no marriage. When a post-nup is created after years of marriage, the threat of "sign it or else there's no wedding" doesn't exist. While a spouse can claim that he was threatened with divorce, it doesn't carry the same weight with the court; it's a threat that can be made regardless of whether a post-nup is signed.

Also, the terms of a prenup generally have to do with property—they're designed to protect the wealth of one spouse and his children. Post-nups are focused first on conduct and second on property. As a result, they're less likely to have provisions that are blatantly unfair in terms of division of property. While continued bad conduct does result in negative sanctions, they should not be egregious or unfair. A good attorney will make sure that the post-nup's terms have the best chance of being enforced under your state's law and that the court will consider them fair.

Alternatives to Traditional Divorce Negotiations

If you were to survey divorced couples and ask them what they thought of the divorce process, many of them would express dissatisfaction. They would complain about their attorneys, about the costs, about the stress, and about the "unfairness" of the settlement terms. Attorneys are acutely aware that pre-divorce couples having problems in their marriages look with suspicion or even downright hostility on the divorce process. Given this awareness, they may well suggest alternatives to divorce when you first meet with them.

These alternatives include counseling, mediation, arbitration, and other methods to help get the marriage back on track or sidestep litigation if a divorce can't be avoided. Attorneys are especially likely to suggest these alternatives to spouses who were the major earners in the family and when they've been married for a number of years. In Illinois and some other states, we're seeing a growing number of cases in which the trend for divorces involving long-term marriages is toward permanent rather than rehabilitative maintenance. The spouse who's the breadwinner may have thought of maintenance as something he would have to pay for two years (which in the past was a common time period for shorter marriages) as his spouse figures out how to start generating income on her own. But now, he's facing the prospect of paying maintenance for ten, twenty, or more years.

An attorney is likely to ask this individual, "Are you sure you want to get a divorce?"

Couples who can't stand each other shouldn't stay together only for financial reasons. Sometimes, the marriage has to end no matter what the cost. But attorneys know that in an environment where divorce is becoming increasingly expensive on many fronts, people are interested in alternatives. Therefore, be prepared for your attorney to suggest some before you file for a divorce. Post-nups, obviously, are one such alternative. But many divorce attorneys now work closely with one or more therapists, and they may suggest seeing a therapist prior to filing for divorce. I believe post-nups are often more effective when therapists are involved in creating them or at least vetting them to make sure that they dovetail with a given couple's situation.

Assess How to Choose and Work with Your Post-Nup Attorney

If you bring an attorney into the process, you need to think about a number of issues and ask your prospective attorney a number of questions. The following will help you do both.

- **Has an attorney you're interviewing done a post-nup before?** Is she familiar with the concept or at least open to this as an alternative approach? Is she an experienced family lawyer who has handled a number of divorces in the past? Is this attorney flexible about using alternatives to the traditional divorce and willing to explore how a post-nup can be used both in trying to save the marriage as well as create a fair settlement if it can't be saved? Is this attorney also willing

---

to be flexible about her work on the post-nup—is she willing to amend a post-nup that you and your spouse create rather than writing it all herself?

- **What is the prospective attorney's estimated fee for working on the post-nup?** Is it considerably less than the cost of even a simple divorce?

- **Have you and your spouse agreed on a single attorney to work with you on the post-nup?** Is one of you willing to be unrepresented as part of this process, or would it make the unrepresented spouse feel more comfortable about the post-nup if he too obtain representation? (I recommend that you each are represented.)

- **Have you (and your spouse) thought about how you will present the post-nup concept to the attorney?** Have you discussed and agreed upon the conduct-related changes that you want to be a part of the post-nup, the negative sanctions if the agreement is violated, and the terms of a divorce?

- **Has your attorney vetted your agreement to make sure it is enforceable under state law?** Has he helped you translate difficult and complex issues into post-nup language that addresses these issues fairly? Has the attorney told you that the post-nup should be updated periodically?

- **If your spouse violates the post-nup agreement, has your lawyer cautioned you about reflexively pulling the divorce trigger?** Has he asked you if you want to revise the agreement to give your spouse one more chance?

- **Have you discussed with your attorney all the alternatives to a traditional divorce, including therapy, mediation, arbitration, and other collaborative tools (including the post-nup)?**

12

When the Marriage
Can't Be Saved

How to Make the Divorce Process Work

LARRY AND ISABEL had been married for twelve years when problems that had been simmering for a while bubbled to the surface. They had a son and daughter, and their son had special needs that required a significant amount of care at a significant financial cost. As time went on, though, Larry endangered their ability to pay for that care because of his gambling. What began as an occasional weekend activity where he'd win or lose a relatively small amount of money became a regular pursuit, and he lost far more than he won. The arguments between Larry and Isabel about his gambling escalated, and Isabel found herself increasingly unhappy in the marriage and concerned about their ability to pay therapists.

Finally, Isabel couldn't deal with the situation anymore and talked to a lawyer. The attorney asked her if she wanted a divorce, and Isabel explained that she only wanted one if Larry continued to gamble. The attorney introduced her to the concept of a postnup, and she thought it would be worth talking with Larry about it. The attorney helped rough out her post-nup agreement and included a clause stipulating that Larry agreed to stop gambling, join Gamblers Anonymous, and attend regular meetings. In the event of a divorce, he would put a sizable amount of money in an escrow account as part of the settlement—this escrow amount would be used to help pay for their son's care if Larry was unable to make his regular support payments.

After some discussion, Larry eventually agreed to these terms and joined Gamblers Anonymous. For two years, he didn't miss a meeting or gamble once. Then, while he was on a business trip, he went with some colleagues to a casino and began gambling again. He stopped attending meetings. When Isabel found out, she contacted her lawyer and filed for divorce. The judge upheld the post-nup agreement and Larry was forced to put money in escrow for their son's care. It turned out this money was needed, because six months after the divorce Larry lost a lot of money in Las Vegas and was unable to meet his support payments for the next four months.

When Isabel and Larry had their initial conversation about the post-nup and signed their agreement, they were hopeful the marriage could be saved; they viewed the behavioral trigger provision as a worst-case scenario clause and trusted that they would never have to use it. Unfortunately, Larry's gambling addiction destroyed the marriage. Fortunately, this provision in the post-nup ensured that their son was able to continue his treatments during the time when Larry lost most of his savings in Las Vegas.

Though the main goal of the post-nup is to help couples resolve their differences and preserve the marriage, this outcome isn't always possible, as this hypothetical story demonstrates. Therefore, you should understand how post-nups also help couples who end up getting divorced.

Post-nups have both obvious and subtle influences on the divorce process. Most obviously, they offer couples a window to discuss issues such as custody, visitation, and division of marital property at a time when they're relatively calm and objective (rather than during a divorce where emotions often trump reason). Less obviously, they provide judges with a pre-divorce agreement that can accelerate the divorce process, saving couples time, money, and stress.

Ideally, you're reading this at a point when your marriage is still salvageable and that is your primary goal. Realistically, however, you should be aware of and prepared for what might happen if the marriage can't be saved, especially given changes in the divorce process.

The Difficulty of Divorce Today

In a way, a post-nup is like divorce insurance; it's a policy you take out against the escalating cost, combativeness, and time commitment that are common elements of twenty-first-century divorces. Many people don't realize how difficult the divorce process has become for couples. They often assume that it will be a similar experience to what a friend or relative went through ten or twenty years ago. In fact, the experience is likely to be much worse due to a number of factors.

Much of the increasing difficulty can be traced to the onset of no-fault divorce laws. These laws were created with the best of intentions, designed to make divorce less acrimonious and less expensive. The results, however, have been mixed at best. While the pre–no fault era had its share of problems, couples, attorneys, and judges knew the rules of the game and so divorces often moved through the courts relatively quickly and with each side knowing what it could and couldn't get. While the idea of assigning blame for a divorce was often illogical and could create animosity, the system had been in place for a long time and all participants were keenly aware that the courts meted out punishment for bad behavior (e.g., having affairs).

No-fault divorce legislation was implemented in the belief that the process would become less expensive and acrimonious if blame were not assigned. As part of the new no-fault system, courts allowed more pretrial discovery, believing that if both parties learned more about each other's case, it would be easier for them to reach an agreement. In fact, the discovery mechanisms fostered additional delays and game-playing. For instance, one side would insist on deposing his client's spouse, creating resentment through the questions asked and the information discovered. One party's attorney may also insist that the children undergo mental health evaluations as part of a custody or visitation strategy and request that the court appoint a child representative to protect the children's interests. This child representative may make recommendations, and if the other side is displeased with these recommendations, they can ask for a new representative to be appointed.

All of this lengthens the process, ratchets up the tension, and increases the cost. Recognizing this unfortunate outcome, the courts have endorsed mediation as a tactic for couples to use, but it also has drawbacks. While mediation does allow spouses to vent and discuss their conflicts and potential agreements, the process can be ineffective—the mediator lacks the authority to forge a binding agreement. While judges possess this authority, they often lack the time to resolve cases—they are swamped in large part because the discovery process has created a backlog of cases and they need to address the oldest ones first. This is especially true in major metropolitan areas, but it is also becoming a problem in smaller jurisdictions (though I practice in the Chicago area, I live in a county with fifty thousand people and it still may take years to resolve many divorce cases there).

With a post-nup in place, however, judges could resolve many cases quickly. Lawyers can present a judge with the post-nup agreement and ask him to review it and determine if it's fair. If the post-nup has been created properly, then it should pass muster and allow the judge to make a ruling after seeing the couple once. Discovery isn't necessary, and the judge is delighted to clear the case quickly.

The post-nup can also moderate the adversarial fervor of the lawyers involved in the case. The increasingly combative nature of divorces isn't just because of issues between couples but is also due to changes in the legal system. It wasn't that long ago that far fewer divorce lawyers existed. Other areas of the law were more lucrative, and so typically a relatively small number of family law specialists in a given area handled a high volume of divorce cases. As a result, a certain collegiality developed among these attorneys, even when they were representing feuding spouses. They knew how to work things out and manage their clients in a way that benefitted a couple—they helped resolve issues with as much speed and as little fighting as possible.

Now, the number of divorce attorneys has multiplied and far less collegiality exists. Some of these attorneys have a gladiator mentality and are all too willing to engage in battle—increasing the cost of divorce. Post-nups can counteract the gladiator effect. With these agreements in place, it is difficult to wage an all-out war because the major issues have already been resolved.

Another complication is legislation that attempts to level the playing field. In many states, legislation mandates that if one spouse makes considerably more money than the other spouse, the lower-earning one can petition the court for divorce attorney fees. This means that some attorneys representing lower-earning spouses may be motivated to take aggressive actions on behalf of their clients, knowing that they stand a better chance of being compensated for their efforts. Before this legislation was passed, these attorneys oper-ated on a fee basis in which the initial retainer might be the only fee that they would receive—they were more likely to try to settle quickly in order to procure a certain (if relatively small) fee rather than drag the process out for two or three years facing an uncertain outcome. Once again, the legislative intention was good (neither spouse should be disadvantaged because they lack resources), but the results were mixed—now both sides may have the dollars to wage divorce war. And once again, post-nups counterbalance this effect, moderating this behavior by putting a divorce agreement in place before the actual divorce process begins.

Finally, post-nups are critical in an era of equality. As I discussed in chapter 3, our legal system has taken steps to create greater equality in the divorce process, reflecting larger trends in society. This is yet another good occurrence with some negative repercussions. Until relatively recently, women tended to accept settlements that reflected the norms of the times—if they received custody and a reasonable amount of alimony, they often accepted a settlement early in the process and without a courtroom battle. Now, they are much more willing and able to assert their rights, challenge settlement offers from their spouses that they feel are unfair, and litigate matters in court.

As pleased as I am by the courts righting past wrongs and creating a more equitable divorce process, these changes to the system require post-nups to counterbalance their negative side effects.

How to Have the Post-Nup Divorce Discussion

This may be the last discussion you want to have while you're working on saving your marriage. You or your spouse may be anxious about even raising the idea of divorce, fearing that once you begin talking about custody, visitation, maintenance, and other matters the divorce will become a *fait accompli*. You may find it much easier talking about the behavior parts of the post-nup—what needs to change in your relationship in order to preserve it. But if these behaviors don't have consequences—outcomes in a divorce settlement—then the post-nup is nothing more than an expression of good intentions.

Therefore, you need to talk about divorce. To facilitate this discussion, here are some suggestions.

• **Position the conversation as a solution rather than as a punishment.** Before introducing the subject of a post-nup to your spouse, consider the context. If the situation is ideal—if your marriage is in decent shape and you're both receptive to this type of discussion—then you probably can discuss divorce outcomes rationally. The more likely scenario, however, is that one spouse's bad behavior is the catalyst for the discussion. This situation means that it's critical to talk about the provisions regarding divorce as solutions—because that's exactly what they can be! If you adopt a do-this-or-else tone, you're likely to catalyze an unproductive argument. Instead, emphasize that this discussion is a far better alternative to the types of battles that take place over kids and property when divorce papers have been filed—that establishing fair terms now will save both of you time, money, and stress if you can't make the marriage work.

In some instances, it's wise to invite an attorney to be part of the discussion. You know your spouse better than anyone, so you can anticipate if he'll react positively, negatively, or indifferently if you suggest a lawyer be present. In either case, an attorney should vet the agreement you create to ensure that a judge will find it fair, but you have to decide when is the right time for his or her involvement.

Be aware that guilt makes people agree to all sorts of unfair things. If you feel guilt about your behavior toward your spouse or your kids, you may agree in a post-nup to give them all your assets if you divorce. Depending on your jurisdiction, a judge may be reluctant to honor this type of division of assets if both you and your spouse have similar incomes and earning potential. If you have a lawyer with you when you're drawing up a post-nup, he would probably protest vehemently against this provision.

- **Cover a range of topics in an innovative, flexible manner.** Don't allow the conversation to become sidetracked on a single issue. For instance, if you become insistent that if your spouse starts drinking again and ignoring you and the children, you will not agree to joint custody or generous visitation if you get divorced, he may become incensed at this possibility and refuse to discuss anything else. Discuss division of property, for instance, or how you'll work out holidays. Instead of getting bogged down on one issue, table that discussion and move on to something else. When you return to this touchy subject, explore alternative sanctions. Be open to his ideas. Together, you should try to think about creative ways to make a divorce as fair and painless as possible.

- **Get the behavioral clauses right.** There are many ways to get them wrong. Perhaps the worst thing you can do is insert a clause that the court will not uphold. For instance, say you stipulate that if your spouse starts using drugs again, his child support payment in the event of a divorce will increase by 25 percent. In many states, courts would invalidate this clause because recommended guidelines are followed and this increase would violate them. Similarly, anything the courts deem unfair will also be thrown out—e.g., losing custody because you missed your child's baseball game.

Being aware of basic divorce laws and recommended guidelines will increase the odds that you will be able to create trigger provision that will stand up under a judge's scrutiny. A lawyer can advise you about these matters, but you should be aware of some basics. Visitation, custody, and maintenance are areas where negotiation room often exists; the courts are likely to uphold less visitation if your spouse's offending behavior involves neglect of the kids, for instance. Best-interest-of-the-child arguments outweigh everything else. Length of the marriage, ages of the spouses, and various situational issues all have an effect on a judge's decision. Clauses in a post-nup need to take these issues into consideration. For example, in long-term marriages where one spouse didn't work for a sustained period of time because she was busy raising the kids, it's difficult to include a clause that fails to provide maintenance or educational assistance because of her behavior. In some states, after twenty or twenty-five years of marriage when a spouse is over a certain age (fifty or fifty-five are common), permanent maintenance or alimony can be presumed until Social Security eligibility. The post-nup can provide reasons that permanent maintenance should not apply to a marriage.

Taking the Post-Nup to Court

If you or your spouse end up filing for divorce, the judge in your case will examine the post-nup and its terms relating to divorce. The more detailed it is in terms of the post-divorce responsibilities and benefits, the easier it will be for the judge to enforce its terms.

The judge is likely to view the post-nup as enforceable as long as the terms are reasonable. You need to convince the judge that the post-nup is a private agreement between two parties rather than crime-and-punishment: you had an affair (crime), therefore I get a divorce and a huge maintenance payment (punishment). Given no-fault laws, adultery cannot be the cause of a divorce—you can't go to court and say something to the effect of, "I'm entitled to a divorce and a lot of money because he cheated on me."

"Fairness" is the critical word in determining the enforceability of post-nups. Azam Nizamuddin is a Chicago attorney and adjunct religion professor at Loyola University, and he is frequently interviewed by the media about issues relating to Islam. He told me about a recent case that is a great illustration of what *not* to include in a post-nup. Uzma Iqbal and Mohammad Khan created a post-nuptial agreement in which they appointed Fisal Hammouda as their "religious and marital counselor and arbiter of their marital affairs." As Azam pointed out, in Islam it's not usual to assign this responsibility to a respected member of the Islamic community (though not necessarily through a post-nup). This practice in and of itself isn't what was unfair about their post-nup. It was that the agreement called for Uzma to forfeit her rights to ownership of their residence if she were to file for divorce without Hammouda's written consent. The post-nup went on to state that if either spouse filed for what Hammouda believed to be an "unreasonable" divorce, that person would forfeit custody rights.

The Illinois Appellate Court ruled that the post-nup was both unconscionable and too ambiguous to be enforceable. It doesn't take a legal scholar to see the unfairness of denying a spouse custody simply because she filed for what a third party deemed an unreasonable divorce. As much as this provision might seem fair to people who grew up in a traditional Islamic community, it comes across as terribly unfair in the Western secular world. Whatever provision you're considering including in your post-nup, therefore, consider whether it will be seen as fair by an objective outsider versus members of your particular community.

The larger issue, of course, is whether judges will be willing to approve a marital settlement with a post-nup at its core, given that post-nups are a relatively new trend. What is the legal justification for upholding a post-nup? Here is the "fairness" logic that a judge might use:

The divorce petition before me doesn't say anything about fault. The parties reached an agreement earlier that strikes me as enforceable. My main job is to determine if the agreement is fair and reasonable for both parties, and it meets these criteria. I understand that the post-nup implies fault but it's not explicit, so I can overlook this implication because the post-nup is structured as a private agreement made at a time prior to the divorce when both parties were thinking clearly, calmly, and fairly about the issues.

Over the next few years, we're likely to see a growing number of post-nups being adjudicated. As judges issue their post-nup-related rulings and opinions and as case law grows, the laws regarding post-nups will evolve accordingly. It's likely, though, that what will evolve is a judicial consensus that if post-nups are fair and agreed to by both parties in a legal document, they will be upheld.

Assessing How a Post-Nup Might Facilitate Your Divorce

At this point, you may still be hopeful of making your marriage work, but conducting an assessment of your situation will provide you with a sense of how a post-nup might benefit you if your marriage does end in divorce. This assessment can also alert you to particular areas that should be major topics during your post-nup discussion with your spouse.

Here are assessment questions to ask yourself about your spouse and about specific concerns you might have if a divorce becomes reality.

> • **How likely is your spouse to change his behavior if you don't have a post-nup with a behavior clause?** Do you believe he needs a clear incentive to change? If he doesn't change, what would be fair compensation in terms of divorce terms?

• **Do you believe your spouse will become angry or vengeful if you seek a divorce?** If you were to file for divorce, might she stop thinking rationally or compassionately and seek terms that are unfair to you and the children? Would she be more likely to agree to fair terms while you're still trying to make the marriage work versus when you know you're going to get divorced?

• **Does a major problem in your marriage have to do with your spouse's addictive behaviors—drinking, drugs, or gambling?** Are you concerned that these behaviors might affect your children adversely, especially if they continue or escalate? Is supervised visitation (for instance) one stipulation that you want your spouse to agree to if he can't stop these addictive behaviors?

• **How might your spouse react when you raise the possibility of a divorce in your post-nup discussion?** Is he more likely to react less angrily if you have an attorney present or conduct the discussion in the attorney's office? Will he react better if you conduct the initial discussion informally, without an attorney present?

• **What do you plan to say to facilitate the most difficult part of the post-nup conversation (the behavior clause)?** How might you frame this discussion as a solution rather than as a punishment? Can you position this clause as being something that will help reduce the cost, stress, and time frame of a divorce?

Thinking about these questions will help you formulate a post-nup discussion strategy and motivate you to bring up the painful possibility of divorce. As important as a post-nup discussion is to establish ground rules that can sustain a marriage, this conversation isn't complete unless behavioral provisions are included.

13

The Need for Post-Nups Now and in the Future

POST-NUPS ARE NOT A TOOL that many married or divorcing couples consider currently, but this situation is bound to change. In both the legal community and society at large, a number of emerging trends suggest that post-nups are going to be an integral part of all types of relationships. As useful as post-nups are today, they are going to be even more valuable in the future due to a series of trends and events. Let's look at some of them and how they will drive adoption of this legal tool.

A Multiplicity of Relationships

Until relatively recently, most people defined their long-term relationships through marriage. Embraced by all types of demographic groups, religions, and the legal system, traditional marriage was a core institution in our society. In fact, until the last fifty years or so, the incidence of divorce was low and it carried a stigma—people who divorced were seen as somehow "less than" those who stayed married, as if they were lacking moral fiber.

Now, though, we're seeing the emergence of many different types of relationships and a growing acceptance in society of these various types. With the divorce rate approaching 50 percent, it's not unusual for people to marry two, three, or more times. As relationships become more diverse and divorce becomes more common, post-nups are more necessary than in the past. Divorce laws as well as the traditional norms that govern marital relationships have become hopelessly outdated. Post-nups provide ground rules for all types of relationships as they facilitate agreements.

Many nontraditional relationship arrangements may require communication about issues different from those that arise in a traditional marriage, and they may also create more complexity if a divorce takes place. For instance, I know of a man who identifies as pan-sexual. He is married (and wishes to remain so) with a family, and he is also a cross-dresser who dates other men and women. As you might imagine, the conversations that he has with his wife are quite a bit different from what a traditional husband and wife discuss; they needed to establish marital rules that are significantly different from the norm for the marriage to survive. If they were ever to get divorced, the settlement too would involve issues that might never arise in the end of a traditional relationship.

Ending a relationship where a couple has had kids together but never married can also be problematic. The couple may have made verbal promises to each other about always staying home with the kids, or that one spouse would always make sure they had health insurance. But if a couple never married, the courts might not view these promises as binding. A post-nup can provide the courts with a document that clearly indicates intent and can increase the odds that a couple's pact will be honored during the paternity court proceedings.

Financial, Legal, and Social Trends

Besides the multiplicity of relationship types, a number of other trends and events are emerging and making post-nups increasingly attractive for couples. Let's look at some of the most significant ones and the effects they're having:

- **The rising cost of divorce.** Post-nups not only lower the odds of divorce (by facilitating better communication), they forge agreements on major divorce-related issues so that if a couple breaks up, costly battles are avoided. Having a post-nup is almost like purchasing divorce insurance; in the event that the worst happens, the post-nup protects you from the financially ruinous battles that characterize adversarial divorces. Periodically, we have couples who call our firm and say something like, "We're getting a divorce but we don't want to spend all the money a divorce usually requires, so can you write up something and we can use that ourselves?" Unfortunately, divorces, like relationships, are complex and without an existing agreement on key issues, it's tough to "write up something" that's effective.

Perhaps just as important, post-nups discourage attorneys from fanning the flames when a divorce client hires them. It's not that divorce attorneys are mercenaries, but that they are trained to fight hard for their clients, and when someone comes to them saying they want a divorce, they reflexively attempt to get the best deal possible. They can convince a client who might have been willing to accept "less" to go to war against her spouse by explaining how the deal her spouse wants isn't fair. When attorneys see that an agreement on key issues has been reached and put in a formal document, they are more likely to accept the post-nup and use that as the basis for a settlement.

- **The rising nonfinancial cost of divorce.** Divorces have become so antagonistic and stressful that many people want an alternative. Just about everyone knows someone who went through a divorce battle, and they know that it can be a horrendous emotional experience. Post-nups take a lot of the emotion and stress out of the process and therefore appeal to people who don't want to become emotional wrecks.

- **Increasing judicial frustration.** Many judges are as eager as couples for divorce alternatives. As we've discussed, they often face daunting decisions involving couples in nontraditional relationships such as gay marriages or blended families. They would like nothing better than having a fair post-nup agreement to guide divorce settlements. While pro se divorces embody the spirit of the post-nup—couples reach settlement agreement on their own—many pro se divorces end up in court post-divorce. Too often, these are ad hoc agreements, forged at the moment of divorce rather than more organically and thoughtfully over the course of the marriage. Consequently, one or both people become unhappy with the settlement shortly after the divorce and they have to hire attorneys and battle out the issues months or even years later.

- **A more collaborative society.** Alliances, joint partnerships, teams, and other collaborative entities are becoming the norm in the business world. The same trend is reflected in the personal sphere, as people form community, religious, and social groups that are diverse rather than homogeneous. In recent years, the concept of a collaborative divorce has gained popularity, and mediation and other less adversarial techniques have become more widely used. Many times, however, these collaborative approaches represent only token nods in the direction of collaboration. Post-nups provide a way to make collaboration integral to both the marital and divorce processes.

- **Less restrictive gender roles.** When I was growing up, my mom would always say, "Your dad is the leader of the family, he's in charge." In fact, she probably made most of the family-related decisions, but she ceded the leadership role to him, as did many women prior to the '70s. Today, men and women may share the roles of breadwinner and head of household. Or they may reverse traditional roles. In either case, it complicates both marriage and divorce. It creates the possibility of many more conflicts during the marriage, and it makes decisions about issues such as custody (when neither spouse was solely in charge of childcare but shared the responsibility equally) more confusing. Post-nups help alleviate much of the confusion.

When Will Post-Nups Become Standard Practice?

It's only a matter of time. It could be as little as a year or two from this writing or it may take five years or a bit longer, but sooner or later, many couples will create a post-nup during the course of their marriage. For all the reasons cited—the trends that are making a collaborative marriage and divorce tool crucial—the time is fast approaching when post-nups become a common sense response to the relationship environment.

Certainly a growing acceptance of this tool in the legal community will stimulate greater usage of post-nups, but the real catalyst will be a grassroots movement. It will be similar to direct-to-consumer pharmaceutical advertising, in which patients see an ad for a given drug and drive usage by requesting that drug from their doctors. In the same way, clients will become aware of post-nups from early adopters and then insist that their lawyers draw up the document for their marriage.

In addition, we're bound to see a surge in publicity for post-nups, just as we've witnessed all the earlier stories about prenups. Invariably, a high profile divorce will feature a post-nup—a celebrity marriage will end in divorce, but it will be an amicable ending because of the post-nup. This media buzz will help educate people about the role a post-nup can play both in saving a marriage and making a divorce less expensive and stressful.

This is also a tool that will likely be embraced by therapists. Traditional marriage counseling is tough, in that couples often come to counseling angry and with their marriages on the rocks. Many therapists will relish having a tool they can give couples that is practical, that can produce options, negotiations, and agreements that can save marriages that are on shaky ground but have strong foundations. These therapists, then, will add another voice that will encourage broader acceptance of this tool.

One potential obstacle exists to post-nups: a minority of divorce lawyers. No doubt, some of them will feel threatened by an agreement that takes some of the power (not to mention some of the money) away from them and puts it in the hands of the couples themselves. They may worry that at least some of their big fee divorces will become small fee ones. Though there will always be a pocket of resistance among family law specialists, I believe that most attorneys truly have the interests of their clients at heart and will recognize that post-nups are an emerging practice area, one that is more like contract law. If the marriage is saved, then there are no legal fees for divorce attorneys, but they can make money by helping to design and update post-nups periodically. They'll still have plenty of traditional divorce work, but post-nups represent an additional practice area that can add to their income. And the attorney can gain the satisfaction of having constructively addressed the problems of a client and, often, saving marriages.

Assess Your Need for a Post-Nup

I'd like to end this book with a self-assessment exercise similar to the ones that have been in previous chapters. This time, however, I'd like to focus the questions on the situations that might make you a good candidate for a post-nup. It's likely that you've considered how a post-nup might help your marriage or facilitate a fair, reduced-stress divorce as you've moved through earlier chapters, but it helps to identify the specific issues that might be resolved or at least managed better through a post-nup.

Therefore, let me leave you with the following questions to reflect upon.

- **Do you have repeated arguments about the same topic with your spouse/partner?** Have these arguments increased in intensity over time, and do they pose a threat to your marriage?

- **Does your relationship with your partner have a complicating factor?** This could include children from a previous marriage, different religions that you both feel strongly about, or clashing values. Are you in a civil union or committed with children but unmarried?

- **If you were to be divorced tomorrow, is it likely that you and your spouse would engage in a pitched battle over custody, visitation, maintenance, and division of community property?**

- **Is your spouse exhibiting some type of addictive behavior—drug or alcohol use or gambling?** Is this behavior creating significant problems in your relationship?

- **Has your spouse had an affair?** Is he currently having one? Are you? Is this causing a rift in your relationship?

- **Were you completely forthcoming about problems from your past when you married your spouse?** If not and if your spouse were to find out about this problem, would it endanger the marriage? If the reverse were the case (your spouse misrepresenting himself), how would you react if you discovered the truth?

- **Have you tried going to counseling to deal with the problems in your relationship?** Has the counseling helped resolve the problems, or do you find that this therapeutic approach lacks "teeth"? Is there too little to motivate your spouse to change his damaging behavior?

- **How motivated would your spouse be to take your complaints and requests seriously if he knew that a failure to do so would result in a divorce and a less favorable divorce settlement?**

Acknowledgments

I want to thank Jim Koch, Lynn Weisberg, John Wrona, and everyone else at Gardiner Koch Weisberg & Wrona for the twenty-five wonderful years that our firm has been serving clients and during which we have worked together as a real team—like no other firm that I know of.

Special thanks to Bruce Wexler for all of his work and counsel and to all the great professionals at Chicago Review Press, especially my excellent editor, Yuval Taylor.

Index